Use It! Don't Lose It!

MATH

Daily Skills Practice
Grade 5

by Pat Alvord

IncentivePublications

Illustrated by Kathleen Bullock
Cover by Geoffrey Brittingham
Edited by Marjorie Frank and Jill Norris
Copyedited by Steve Carlon

ISBN 978-0-86530-664-6

2   3   4   5   6   7   8   9   10   10

Printed by Sheridan Books, Inc., Chelsea, Michigan • September 2010
www.incentivepublications.com

Don't let those math skills get lost or rusty!

As a teacher you work hard to teach math skills to your students. Your students work hard to master them. Do you worry that your students will forget the material as you move on to the next concept?

If so, here's a plan for you and your students—one that will keep those skills sharp.

Use It! Don't Lose It! provides daily math practice for all the basic skills. There are five math problems a day, every day for 36 weeks. The skills are correlated to national and state standards.

Students practice all the fifth-grade skills, concepts, and processes in a spiraling sequence. The plan starts with the simplest level of fifth-grade skills, progressing gradually to higher-level tasks, as it continually circles around and back to the the same skills at a little higher level, again and again. Each time a skill shows up, it has a new context—requiring students to dig into their memories, recall what they know, and apply it to another situation.

The Weekly Plan — Five Problems a Day for 36 Weeks

Monday – Thursday ....
- one computation item (whole numbers, fractions, decimals, or integers)
- one problem-solving task (word problem)
- one measurement problem

Monday and **Wednesday** ......
- one statistics or probability item
- one geometry item

Tuesday and **Thursday** ....
- one number concepts item
- one item using algebra concepts

Friday ....
- two computation items
- one number concepts item
- one item rotating among math strands
- one *Challenge Problem* demanding more involved steps, thinking skills, and calculations (making use of several skills)

Contents

36 Weeks of Daily Practice, five problems a day.. 5–112

Scope and Sequence Charts of Skills, Concepts, Processes 113–118
    (all the details of what's covered, where, and when)

Answer Key 119–127

How to Use Daily Skills Practice

To get started, reproduce each page, slice the Monday–Thursday lesson pages in half, or prepare a transparency. The lessons can be used . . .

- **for independent practice**—Reproduce the lessons and let students work individually or in pairs to practice skills at the beginning or end of a math class.
- **for small group work**—Students can discuss and solve the problems together and agree on answers.
- **for the whole class review**—Make a transparency and work through the problems together as a class.

Helpful Hints for Getting Started

- Though students may work alone on the items, always find a way to review and discuss the answers together. In each review, ask students to describe how they solved the problem-solving problems or other problems that involve choices of strategies.

- Allow more time for the Friday lesson. The Challenge Problem may take a little longer. Students can work in small groups to discover good strategies and correct answers for this problem.

- Provide measurement tools and other supplies students need for solving the problems. There will not be room on the sheet for all problems to be solved. Students will need scratch paper for their work.

- Decide ahead of time about the use of calculators. Since the emphasis is on students practicing their skills, it is recommended that the items be done without calculators and other calculation aids. If you want to focus specifically on technology skills, set a particular goal for certain lessons to be done or checked with calculators. You might allow calculator use for the Friday Challenge Problems.

- The daily lessons are designed to be completed in a short time period, so that they can be used along with your regular daily instruction. However, don't end the discussion until you are sure all students "get it," or at least until you know which ones don't get something and will need extra instruction. This will strengthen all the other work students do in math class.

- Keep a consistent focus on the strategies and processes for problem solving. Encourage students to explore and share different approaches for solving the problems. Explaining (orally or in writing) their problem-solving process is an important math skill. Be open to answers (correct ones, of course) that are not supplied in the Answer Key.

- Take note of which items leave some or all of the students confused or uncertain. This will alert you to which skills need more instruction.

- The daily lessons may include some topics or skills your students have not yet learned. In these cases, students may skip items. Or, you might encourage them to consider how the problem could be solved. Or, you might use the occasion for a short lesson that would get them started on this skill.

1. Solve the problem.

$$325 + 416 = 741$$

2. On Monday, the Miller family traveled 130 miles from their home in Indianapolis to Splashin' Safari. They drove 75 miles before breakfast. How many miles did they drive after breakfast?

55 miles

3. Find the mean (average) number of rides for the four children.

11

Number of Rides Taken on July Fourth at Knott's Berry Farm: Sara 11, Keith 16, Megan 9, Reggie 8

4. The diameter of many Ferris wheels is 50 feet. Draw a red line to show the diameter of the Ferris wheel at the right. Label it 50 ft.

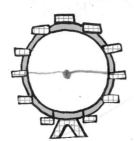

5. Hank Wiley needs to pay for himself, his nine-year-old twins, and his four-year-old. Calculate his admission cost.

$59.85

Add it up!

TICKETS TO ROCKLAND PARK

Adults & Children (over 10)
$39.95

Children 5-9
$9.95

Children Under 5
FREE

1. More than three hundred twenty-eight million people visit an amusement park in the United States each year. Which of the following shows that numeral?

　a. 3,000,028 　　c. 3,028,000
　b. 328,000,000 　d. 328,000

2. Solve the problem.

$$6 \times \boxed{7} = 42$$

3. It was 78 degrees Fahrenheit at 10:00 a.m. when Jamie's family arrived at Six Flags Amusement Park. By noon the temperature had risen 16 degrees. How warm was it at noon?

94 degrees

4. Solve the problem.　**568**
　　　　　　　　　　+ 341
　　　　　　　　　　909

5. Shawn has $6.50 to spend for lunch. He plans to buy at least three items. Describe two different lunches he might buy.

Dino Dogs w/chili
Neander nachos
lg Jungle Juice

ROCKLAND PARK DINO CAFE

Steggy Burgers...........$2.75
Dino Dogs..................$2.25
Dino Dogs w/chili......$2.50
Raptor Fries...............$2.00
Neander-nachos........$1.75
Dactyl Chips..............$0.75
Ice Man Bars.............$2.00
Jungle Juice
sm. $1.00　　med. $1.25　　lg. $1.50

1. Which is the right angle?

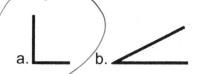

a.   b.   c.

2. Of 100 people surveyed, 82 visited an amusement park last year. How many did not visit an amusement park?

18 People

3. Solve the problem.

408 + 126 + 374 = 908

4. Margo's family got in line for the Magic Mountain ride at 10:06 a.m. It was their turn to ride at 10:54 a.m. How long did they wait in line?

48 min

5. Ben wants two different flavors on his double dip cone. Draw a picture to show how many different choices he has.

10 choices

TODAY'S FLAVORS

Fudge Swirl (F)
Berry Ripple (B)
Cookie Dough (C)
Rocky Road (R)
Mint Chip (M)

1. A person must be four feet tall to ride the Cyclone roller coaster. Shane is 50 inches tall. Is he tall enough?

Yes

2. Round each of the following numerals to the nearest hundred.

a. 516   500
b. 187   200
c. 308   300

3. Solve the problem.

867 − 423 = 444

4. Find a number that when multiplied by 5 gives a product of 45.

a. 9   c. 6
b. 12   d. not here

5. What missing information is needed to solve the problem?

The members of the Bakerville Scout Troop each paid $4.75 to visit the Fun House. What was the total cost of their admission?

How many students were there?

We had a blast!
Troop #4

Admission Total:
_____

Name

1. The Morris family of five will each spend $29.95 for a day-long ticket to Adventure Land. _About_ how much money will their family spend on admission?

$150

2. Place these numbers in order from greatest to least.

1175   1751   1715   1157

1   3   4   2

3. Coney Island's **Thunderbolt** roller coaster operated from 1925 until 2000. How many years was it in operation?

75 years

4. The world's largest Ferris wheel in Yokohama, Japan has 60 gondolas. Each gondola holds 8 people. How many people can ride the Ferris wheel at a time?

60

5. Challenge Problem

An amusement park named Thrills & Chills conducted a survey of adult visitors to learn which ride they preferred. 46% liked the rollercoaster; 13% preferred the bumper cars; 10% the log flume; 9% the Ferris wheel and 7% the carousel. The rest were undecided about their favorite ride.

a. What percentage of people could not decide on their favorite ride? ___15 Percent___

b. Create a bar graph that communicates this information.

Title: ___Thrills and chills___

Color the bar graph.

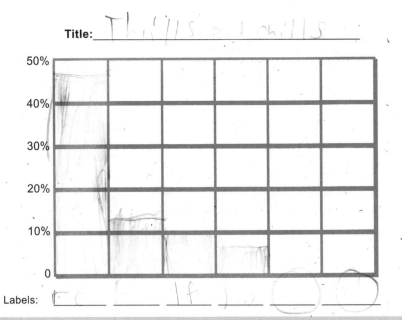

Labels: ___

1. Hurricanes are serious storms that begin over tropical waters. If the wind speed stays under 73 miles per hour, the storm will just be considered a tropical storm. If the speed exceeds that amount, the storm is called a hurricane. A particular tropical storm in the Caribbean Sea has a wind speed of 54 miles per hour. How much must the wind speed increase before the storm is called a hurricane?

2. Solve the problem.   **5.6 + 7.9 =**

3. What are your chances of tossing an even number?

4. A hurricane warning is announced at least 18 hours before the storm is expected in your area. If a warning is issued at 5:00 a.m., when should you be prepared for it to strike?

11:00

5. Notice the dotted line of symmetry on each of the following figures.

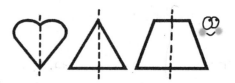

a. Which of the letters on the hurricane message below have one line of symmetry? ___A, R, B___

b. Which letters have no line of symmetry? ___E, L, A___

c. Do any of the letters have more than one line of symmetry? ___yes___

BE ALERT

1. Each year, hurricane season begins on June 1st and ends on November 30th. What is the best estimate of the number of days in hurricane season?

   a. 200 days

   b. 120 days

   c. 180 days

2. Rewrite this expression using words.

   y x 9 = 18

   y x eighteen

3. A family should store two quarts of water for each family member for each day of the storm. How many quarts would a family of six need for a storm that might last three days?

   12 quarts

4. What is the value of the 6 in this numeral?

   5,675.34

   hundredths

5. Julie and her dad will prepare for a possible hurricane by covering their windows with pieces of plywood. Use the formula for area (length times width) to see how many square feet of plywood are needed to cover this window.

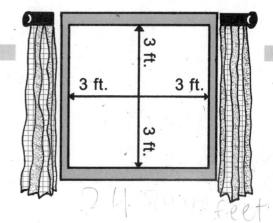

24 square feet

1. The local weather station in Stormville gives hurricane updates every six minutes. At this rate, how many updates would the weather station give in: a. 1 hour _60_? b. 2 hours _120_?

2. Solve the problem. $29 - 16.3 =$

3. Most hurricanes that hit the United States strike the coastline between Texas and Maine. Dione spends all of his summers and falls in southern California. What is the likelihood of his experiencing a hurricane?
   a. highly unlikely
   b. quite likely
   c. impossible to know

4. What geometric figure comes next?

5. Meteorologists measure the wind speed of hurricanes and put them into categories.

   a. What is the difference between the wind speed of the mildest category 1 hurricanes and the worst category 4 hurricanes?

   b. What is the difference between the least and greatest wind speeds of a category 2 hurricane?

Hurricane Speeds

Category	Miles Per Hour
1	74–95
2	96–110
3	110–130
4	131–155
5	155+

THURSDAY WEEK 2 _____
Name

MATH PRACTICE

1. Find the value of **s** if **m** = 21.

   $s + m = 46$

2. The Rodriguez family bought 60 yards of rope to secure their boat to the pier in preparation for a storm. How many feet of rope did they purchase?

3. Solve the problem.

   $144 \div 9 =$

4. Draw a line to match each fraction with the decimal of equal value.

   a. $\frac{1}{4}$ 0.5
   b. $\frac{1}{2}$ 0.25
   c. $\frac{3}{4}$ 0.75

5. Marika and Matt helped their elderly neighbors prepare for the hurricane. Matt worked from 8:50 a.m. until 11:20 a.m. Marika worked from 9:20 a.m. until noon.

   a. Estimate their total amount of time.

   b. Calculate their exact amount of time.

   c. Evaluate your estimate:
   very close _____
   fairly close _____
   way off _____

Nice calculation!

It's time to get busy.

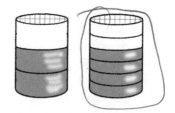

1. The diagrams to the right have equal parts shaded.
Write the fraction that describes each figure.
Then circle the fraction that is in lowest terms.

2. What is 5 less than 4 times 7?   4×7=28

3. Which is an example of the commutative (order) property?
   a. (6 + 5) + 2 = 6 + (5 + 2)
   b. 3(6 + 4) = (3 × 6) + (3 × 4)
   c. 3 + 4 = 4 + 3

I hope I can
weather the storm!

4. Anthony has the following change in his right pocket:
2 quarters, 3 dimes, and 2 nickels. How much money is this?

90¢

5. Challenge Problem

Rachel is making gorp to store up in bags for hurricane season. She has this recipe, but wants to double it.

   a. Finish the table with the correct amounts.
   b. There are 4 cups in a quart. How many quarts of gorp will she have? _____
   c. Rachel will divide the gorp into zipper storage bags with $\frac{1}{2}$ cup per bag.
      How many bags can she make? _____

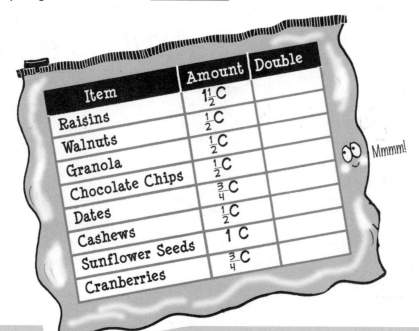

Item	Amount	Double
Raisins	$1\frac{1}{2}$ C	
Walnuts	$\frac{1}{2}$ C	
Granola	$\frac{1}{2}$ C	
Chocolate Chips	$\frac{1}{2}$ C	
Dates	$\frac{3}{4}$ C	
Cashews	$\frac{1}{2}$ C	
Sunflower Seeds	1 C	
Cranberries	$\frac{3}{4}$ C	

Mmmm!

Name

1. Yellowstone National Park has 1,200 miles of hiking trails. Which sets of factors have a product of 1,200?

   a. 12 x 100 b. 120 x 10 c. 12 x 1,000

2. The wolf heads are:
   a. similar
   b. congruent

3. The geyser, Old Faithful, erupts about every 75 minutes. At this rate how many eruptions would you expect to see in 4 hours?

3.2

4. What is the range between the highest and lowest eruption heights of the three geysers?

GEYSER	Height of Steam & Water at Eruptions
STEAM BOAT	120 METERS
GIANT	60 METERS
OLD FAITHFUL	50 METERS

5. Use a ruler. Measure each of the following line segments to the nearest centimeter.

   a. ___2 Cm___
   b. ___5 Cm___
   c. ___3 Cm___

a

b

c

I love to measure.

(student work shown: 75 × 2 = 150; 75 × 3 = 225; 75)240(3.2; 225; 150; 150; 0)

Name

1. What would be the total fee for two days of camping at Lewis Lake ($10 per night) and one at Grant Village ($15 per night)?

10+15=$25

Lewis Lake

GRANT VILLAGE

2. Solve the problem. Be sure to place the decimal point in the correct place.

   4.2
   x 6.8

   33.6   285.6

3. The speed limit in Yellowstone National Park is 45 miles per hour. At this rate, about how long would it take a car to drive the 140-mile loop around the park?

3.1

(student work: 45 × 3 = 135; 45)140(3.1...; 135; 50; 45; 50)

4. Solve the equation. Do the operation in the ( ) first.

   (15 + 8) + 9 = 32

   23
   + 9
   32

5 Use the scale to figure the height of an average adult male grizzly bear.

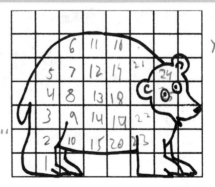

Scale: side of square = 6"

152

(student work: 25 × 6 = 150)

1. What is the difference in weight between the largest male and the largest female grizzly bear?

300

2. Use the chart to calculate the mean (average) weight for adult grizzly bears.

    a. average female weight _____

    b. average male weight _____

ADULT GRIZZLY BEAR WEIGHT		
	Minimum Adult Weight	*Maximum Adult Weight*
MALE	300 LBS	700 LBS
FEMALE	200 LBS	400 LBS

3. Yellowstone Park celebrated its 50th birthday in 1922.

*1922
− 50
1872*

    a. When was the park created? _1872_

    b. How old is Yellowstone now? _141_

4. Solve the problem.

*2013
−1872
141*

    847 + 683 = _141_

*847
+ 683
930*

5. Which shape is congruent to figure a?

a   b   c   d

1. Humans are the greatest threat to the survival of Yellowstone Park's wolves. They are responsible for one-half of wolf deaths. If 14 wolves are killed in one season, how many deaths did people probably cause?

*1
14
× 4
56*

56

2. Round to the nearest whole number. **124.3**

124

I'm going camping.

3. Tower Falls Campground has an elevation of 6,600 feet. How many yards high is the campground?

2,200

4. Which equation has ***not*** been solved correctly?

    a. 9 + p = 16 (p = 9)

    b. 12 − r = 7 (r = 5)

5. Use the table to answer the questions.

*7800
−6900
900*

    a. What is the difference between the elevation of Lewis Lake Campground and Pebble Creek Campground? _900_

900

    b. What is the total number of campsites at Indian Creek, Mammoth, and Grant Village?

585   *75   160
+ 85 + 425*

    c. What is the difference between the least and most expensive campground fees? _$19_

*−29
−10
19*

YELLOWSTONE CAMPGROUND SITE

	Fees	Sites	Elev (ft)
Fishing Bridge RV	$29	346	7,800
Grant Village	$15	425	7,800
Indian Creek	$10	75	7,300
Lewis Lake	$10	85	7,800
Mammoth	$12	85	6,200
Pebble Creek	$10	32	6,900

1. Bob and Jody Harrison will take the Grand Loops Tour with their two children Lela, age 15, and Lionel, age 10. They calculated their cost to be $144.60. Check their accuracy.

My answer is $145.60

2. The tour lasts nine and one-half hours. At what time will the Harrisons complete their trip?

6:00

3. After traveling the first 62 miles the bus will stop so the tourists can enjoy a picnic lunch. How many miles will the bus travel after lunch?

78 miles

```
  140
-  62
   78
```

4. Twenty-five percent of the 72 passengers on today's Grand Loops Day-Long Tour will ride free. How many children (under 12) will be on the tour?

47 children

```
  72
- 25
  47
```

Yellowstone-in-a-Day, Inc.
Grand Loops Day-Long Tour
- Travel 140 miles around the park -

Departure Time: 8:30 a.m.

Departure Location:
    Mammoth Hot Springs Hotel

Cost:

    Adult........................$58.24
    Age 12-16..............$29.12
    11 and under.........Free

```
   58.24
x  
  117.48
```

```
  116.48
+  29.12
  145.60
```

---

5. Challenge Problem

Study the table of information.

   a. Create a line graph to show the information on the chart. Add a title and labels.

   b. What trend does the graph tell you about the number of tourists taking the tour on July 4th?

   c. If the trend continued, how many visitors took the tour in 2006? *Ans: 233*

Title: *Yellowstone-in-a-Day*

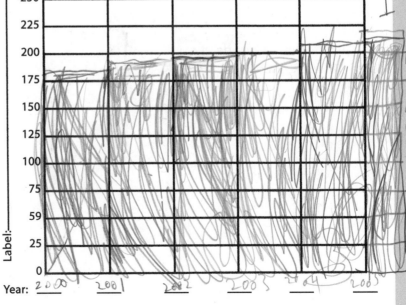

Yellowstone-in-a-Day Number of Tourists

July 4th -	Number
2000	176
2001	183
2002	191
2003	200
2004	210
2005	221

I love a challenge.

```
  221
+  12
  233
```

I dont know how to make a line graph but I am making a Bar Graph

MONDAY WEEK 4 <u>Ani</u>

1. The Yokohama Bay Bridge in Tokyo, Japan is 860 meters long. Which is true about the length of the bridge?

   a. It is greater than a kilometer long.

   b. It is less than a kilometer long.

   c. It is just about a kilometer long.

2. Solve the problem.

au

$$94 - \underline{21} = 73$$

-73
21

Measure up.

3. With eyes closed, you pick up one card from a set of alphabet letters. What are your chances of picking up a card with a vowel?

Unlikely

4. The London Bridge was built in 1209 and lasted 600 years. In what year was the bridge destroyed?

1809

1209
+ 600
1809

5. The ancient Greeks invented arch bridges. Which geometric shape most resembles an arch?

   a. hemisphere

   b. sphere

   c. cone

   d. semicircle

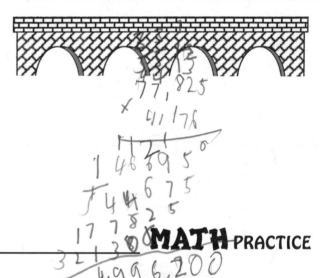

77,825
× 41,176

148 950
44 675
17 7 825
32 1 3 0
33,4,996,200

TUESDAY WEEK 4 _____

1. Solve by subtracting. Then check by adding.

305
-192

113

1
113
+192
305

2. The bridge over Trevor's backyard stream is six feet long and three feet wide. What is the area of the bridge?

18 sf

3. Which is a prime number? *(Hint: A prime number has only two factors—itself and 1.)*

 6 114  9 10 **3**

4. The Verrazano Narrows Bridge is 4,176 meters long and was built at a cost of $77,825 per meter. Use a calculator to figure the total cost of the bridge.

4413
77,825

$334,996,200

5. Fact: The Golden Gate Bridge is 1.2 miles long.

Fact: There are 5,280 feet in one mile.

Which equation would you use to find out the length of the bridge in feet?

   a. 5,280 x 1.2=

   b. 5,280 ÷ 1.2 =

   c. 5,280 – 1.2

   d. Not Here

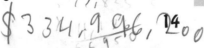

1. Find the next three numbers in the pattern.

4, 12, 36, _52_ , _74_ , _102_

16 + 22 +28
52   74   102

2. The longest floating bridge is located in Seattle, Washington and is 2.39 miles long. At 9:25 a.m., some students began a one hour and twenty-five minute hike across the bridge. What time did they reach the other side?

10:50

3. Solve the problem.

1 2 3
3⟌369
36
00
0

4. What is the chance of randomly choosing a day of the week that begins with the letter "T"?

unlikly

5. Plot each of the following ordered pairs on the graph to create the outline of a bridge. Connect the dots in order.

(0, 3), (1, 5), (1, 3), (2, 5), (2, 3), (3, 5), (3, 3, (4, 5), (4, 3), (5, 5), (6, 3), (6, 5), (7, 3), (7, 5), (8, 3), (8, 5), (9, 3), (9, 5), (10, 3)

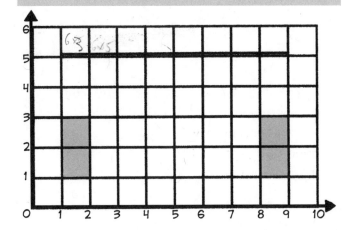

1. Rainbow Bridge, located in Utah, is the world's highest natural arch. It is 82.3 meters long and 88.4 meters high. What is the difference between the arch's height and length?

2. Simplify. Then find the sum if m = 11.

3m + 2m + 1m =

3. Which is an example of the associative (grouping) property?

a. (a + b) + c = (a + b + c)

b. a + b + c = c + b + a

c. (a + b) + c = a + (b + c)

4. The perimeter of the scalene triangle is 22 meters. Find the length of the missing side.

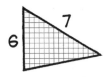

5. Number the bridges in order from shortest to longest.

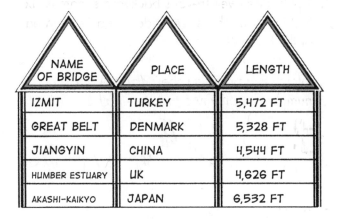

NAME OF BRIDGE	PLACE	LENGTH
IZMIT	TURKEY	5,472 FT
GREAT BELT	DENMARK	5,328 FT
JIANGYIN	CHINA	4,544 FT
HUMBER ESTUARY	UK	4,626 FT
AKASHI-KAIKYO	JAPAN	6,532 FT

1. Notice the pattern. Then solve the equation.

$4 \times 2 = 8$ $4 \times 20 = 80$

$4 \times 200 = 800$ $4 \times 2,000 = \underline{8000}$

2. Estimate the answer by rounding.

$39 \times 24 =$

a. 60   c. 1,200

b. 600   d. 800

3. A class of 27 students will be divided into three-person teams for a bridge-building contest. How many teams will there be?

4. Use a colored marker to trace these geometric features in the picture of the Millau Bridge.

a. an acute angle

b. parallel lines

c. a line segment

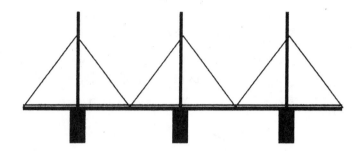

5. Challenge Problem

Peter, Ben, Amber, and Chelsea brought plastic drinking straws to school for a bridge building project. Peter brought fewer than Ben and Amber but more than Chelsea. Ben brought 15 more than Amber. Chelsea brought one-third as many as Peter. Amber has 11 less than twice as many as Peter. Together they brought 89 straws. How many did each person bring?
(Hint: Begin by making a guess about the number of straws Chelsea brought.)

$B = 15$

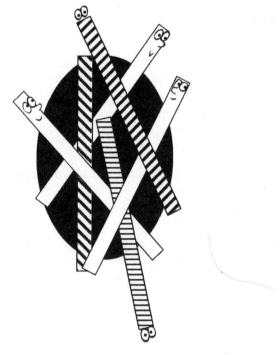

MONDAY WEEK 5 _____ MATH PRACTICE
Name

1. Jason and Jane were comparing the amount of orange juice they each drank in one week. Jason said, "I had twelve eight-ounce glasses of juice!" Jane's response was, "What's the big deal? I drank three quarts of juice!" Who drank the most?

(handwritten:) 12 ×8   96 ounces   4×3=12 cups Jane   3×4=12 Jasonq 96oz=3 quarts

2. Solve the problem. $\frac{1}{8} + \frac{3}{8} + \frac{4}{8} =$

3. In a box of Energy Bars, five are oatmeal raisin, three are apple cinnamon, and four are date apricot. If you grab one bar without looking, what are the chances it will be a date apricot?

(handwritten:) $\frac{4}{12} = \frac{1}{3}$

4. Give a label to the center of this Venn Diagram.

(handwritten labels: apple, Fruits, Orange)

5. Draw a line to match each food picture with the word that describes its geometric figure.

a. cylinder

b. sphere

c. hemisphere

d. cone

e. rectangular prism

f. triangular prism

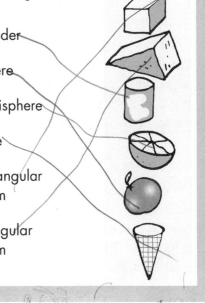

TUESDAY WEEK 5 _____ MATH PRACTICE
Name

1. Write as a standard numeral:

   30,000 + 2,000 + 100 + 4 = *(handwritten:)* 32,104

2. Which equation matches the statement?

   Guess my number. If I add 6 to it and multiply the sum by 3, my answer will be 33.

   a. (6 x 3) + n = 33   c. (n x 6) + 3 = 33
   b. 33 = n − 6   d. (n + 6) x 3 = 33

3. Add the correct symbol: **<, >,** or **=**.

   (6 x 8) + 1 ☐ **9 x 5**

4. How much is saved by buying one gallon of Dairyland milk instead of two half gallons?

   DAIRYLAND MILK
   $1.89 GALLON
   $0.98 HALF GALLON
   $0.50 QUART

5. Find the weight of this bunch of bananas. Write the answer in pounds and ounces. *(Hint: There are 16 ounces in a pound.)*

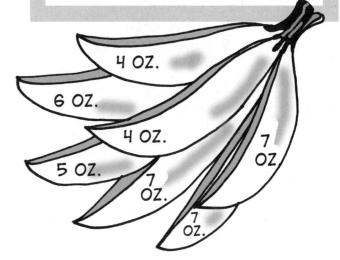
4 OZ.   6 OZ.   4 OZ.   5 OZ.   7 OZ.   7 OZ.   7 OZ.

Use It! Don't Lose It! IP 613-0

WEDNESDAY WEEK 5 _____ MATH PRACTICE

Name

1. Which statement defines the statistical term "mode?"
   a. the difference between the greatest and smallest number on the list
   b. the average of the numbers on the list
   c. the number in the middle of a list a numbers
   d. the number that appears most often on the list.

2. Middle grades kids should have at least two cups of vegetables each day. So far today, Kim has had $\frac{2}{3}$ of a cup of sliced cucumbers. How much more does she need to meet the requirement?

3. Find the error. Then write the correct answer.

4. What is the volume of the granola box? *(Hint: To find volume, multiply length by width by height.)*

GRANOLA
8 IN.
2 IN.
6 IN.

$$593$$
$$-149$$
$$\overline{456}$$

593
-149
444

96 in

$\frac{3}{3} = 4c$

$\frac{7}{3} = 2\frac{1}{3}$

$\frac{6}{3} = 2$

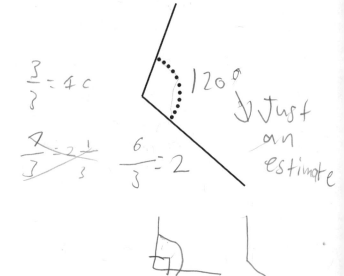

$120°$ ↓ Just an estimate

5. Use a protractor to measure the obtuse angle.

THURSDAY WEEK 5 _____ MATH PRACTICE

Name

1. What is the ratio of raisins to peanuts?

(Hint: You can write a ratio as a fraction!)

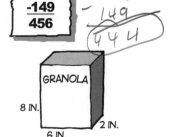

$\frac{12}{18} = \frac{2}{3}$

2. Solve the problem. **24.6 – 18.9 =** 5.7

$$-24.6$$
$$18.9$$
$$\overline{5.7}$$

3. Most middle grades kids need 2,200 calories each day. So far Jonathan has eaten 1,848 calories. How many calories can he still have today?

352 Calories

$$2,200$$
$$1,848$$
$$\overline{352}$$

4. Solve the equation if $s = 9$

   $(s \times 3) + 7 =$ 34

5. Brittany wants to triple the recipe to serve herself and two friends. How much of each ingredient will she need?

4 ice cubes

Recipe
Scrumptious Smoothie (1 serving)

$\frac{1}{2}$ CUP PLAIN LOW FAT YOGURT
$\frac{1}{3}$ OF A BANANA
$\frac{1}{4}$ CUP OF SLICED STRAWBERRIES
$\frac{1}{4}$ CUP LOW FAT MILK
   4 ICE CUBES
      MIX ALL IN A BLENDER

1. During the week of September 24, the Riverdale School cafeteria offered a soup and salad lunch choice to students. These are the numbers of students who chose this lunch during the week:

Monday – 70	
Tuesday – 60	
Wednesday – 40	
Thursday – 75	
Friday – 90	

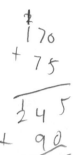

$$170$$
$$+ 75$$
$$\overline{245}$$
$$+ 90$$
$$335$$

   a. What was the range between the lowest and highest number of soup-salad lunches sold?

   75

   b. What is the total number of soup and salad lunches sold during the week?

   335

2. When the cooks checked their records, they noticed that the number of soup and salad lunches sold on all four Mondays in the month was the same. What was the total number of lunches sold on Mondays during this particular month?

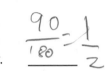

3. Riverdale School has 180 students. Write a fraction (in lowest terms) to show how many students chose soup and salad on Friday.

   $$\frac{90}{180} = \frac{1}{2}$$

   Now write that fraction as a percent.

   % 90

4. A gallon of soup serves 15 students. How many gallons of soup were used on Thursday?

   15 gallons

5. Challenge Problem

Mario's mom set out the following sandwich supplies and told him to make his lunch. How many different ways can he make a sandwich? Draw a tree diagram to solve.

Wheat - W	
Sourdough - S	
Turkey - T	
Ham - H	
Cheddar Cheese - CC	
Swiss Cheese - SC	

Sandwich Choices:
Wheat bread and sourdough bread; turkey and ham; and cheddar and swiss cheese.

1. The course of the Mississippi River was changed in 1812 when Missouri had a small earthquake. How many years ago was the course changed?

2. Estimate the sum.

$$586 + 329 + 12 =$$

3. In the summer of 2002, Martin Strel swam the entire length of the Mississippi River. He began on July 4 and finished on September 9. How many days did it take him to swim the 2,360 miles?

4. Since the angle above the line AD must measure 180 degrees, what is the measurement of angle CBD?

110°

A   B   D

C

5. Use the information on the table to create a question that requires ONE math operation. Be sure to give the correct answer.

The World's Five Longest Rivers

river	mi	k
Nile	4,160	6,695
Amazon	4,007	6,448
Yangtze	3,964	6,378
Mississippi	3,870	6,228
Ob	3,460	5,570

1. The Bensons will vacation on the Colorado River for two weeks, and plan to raft six hours each day. How many hours in all will they spend rafting?

2. Solve the problem. $438 \times 5 =$

3. Which property is demonstrated here?

$$3,455 \times 1 = 3,455$$

4. Which equation would you use to find the difference between the length of the Amur and Huang Rivers?

a. $4,415 - 4,400 =$ c. $5,464 - 4,400 =$

b. $5,464 + 4,415 =$ d. $5,464 - 4,415 =$

river	length (km)
Huang	5,464
Amur	4,415
Lena	4,400

5. Which is the best estimate of the length of this line segment?

a. 5 cm

b. 8 cm

c. 6 cm

d. 7 cm

That's a great line.

WEDNESDAY WEEK 6 _____ MATH PRACTICE
Name

1. Write this as an exponential number.

3 x 3 x 3 x 3 x 3

2. Think! How can you tell there will be no remainder?

Solve the problem.

$3 \overline{)324}$

3. The average winter temperature along Idaho's Snake River is 29 degrees F. What would the temperature be if an unusual cold front caused it to drop 32 degrees below normal?

4. Circle the median number on the list.

39   34   46   28   43   24   42

5. Add the line segments necessary to complete a cube.

I'm not a square, I'm a cube.

THURSDAY WEEK 6 _____ MATH PRACTICE
Name

1. The Rio Grande River is 3200 kilometers long. Multiply that by 1,000 to find the length of the river in meters.

2. Write these decimals in order from greatest to least.

35.1   32.6   34.06   36.2   30.48

3. Thirty-five percent of the wind surfers on the Columbia River last summer were between the ages of 18 and 30. If 420 people surfed on a July day, how many were between 18 and 30?

4. Use the formula to find the circumference of Margo's inner tube.

32 inches

(Circumference = 3.14 x diameter)

5. Complete the function table—fill in the blanks in the second canoe.

Weekly Rafting
Rule: Afternoon Rafters = Morning + 12

Morning River Rafters

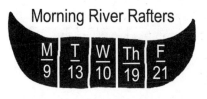

M	T	W	Th	F
9	13	10	19	21

Afternoon River Rafters

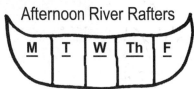

M	T	W	Th	F

1. Find the value of 2^4.

2. Which of the fractions is equivalent to (the same as) $\frac{3}{8}$?

    a. $\frac{6}{16}$ c. $\frac{1}{2}$

    b. $\frac{6}{4}$ d. $\frac{2}{3}$

4. Solve:

$$3.25 - 0.08 = \underline{\quad\quad}$$

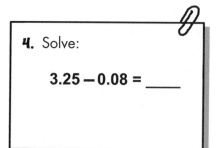

Oops!

scratch scratch

3. Kevin got ready for a canoe trip on the Missouri River by paddling every day for five days before the trip. On Monday he paddled 25 minutes. If he added 5 minutes to his workout every day, how much time did he spend preparing?

_____ hours _____ minutes

5. Challenge Problem

The members of the River Lovers Club took a survey to see how people best like to spend their time on a lazy river. Here's what they learned: 30 preferred kayaking; 10 inner tubing; 5 canoeing; 40 riding on inflatable rafts; and 15 floating in a life jacket.

    a. Design a table that communicates this information.

    b. Display the information on the pie graph below.

I'm looking for the Leaky Tub Team.

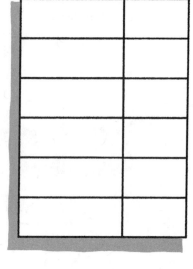

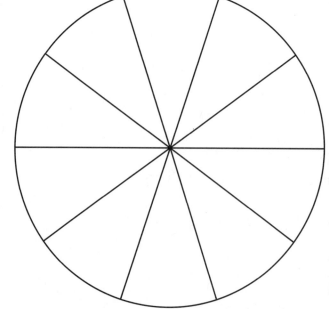

1. Students in the Future Pilots Club were comparing the number of times they'd flown on jumbo jets. What is the mean number of flights for the club members?

Sam 3   Meg 6   Peter 3   Amber 6

Jesse 4   Justin 2   Sarah 4

2. Add the correct symbol to make the statement true: **<**, **>**, or **=**.

(54 ÷ 9) – 6 ☐ **(81 ÷ 9) – 8**

3. Underline the information necessary for solving the problem.

Ryan's family will fly from Portland, OR to San Diego, CA over winter break. They'll wake up at 5:30 a.m. in order to check in by 7:30 for their flight that will take 2 hours and 47 minutes. It takes 50 minutes to drive from home to the airport. When should they leave home?

4. Find the perimeter of this parallelogram.

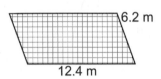

6.2 m

12.4 m

5. Find the area of the picture frame.

14 in.

9 in.

1. What is the most realistic estimate of the weight of the duffel bag?

   a. 15 g
   b. 1.5 kg
   c. 150 g
   d. 8 kg

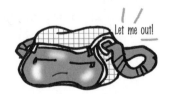

Let me out!

2. Circle all the composite numbers in the set. *(Hint: Composite numbers have more than two factors.)*

   3   11   7   9   4   15   6   5

3. Solve the problem.

   $3\overline{)7.05}$

4. Write the next three numbers in the pattern.

   50, 49, 47, 44, 40, ____, ____, ____

5. Which two equations could you use to solve the problem?

   A jet that can handle 130 passengers has 23 empty seats. How many people are on the flight?

   a. 130 + 23 =
   b. 23 + ____ = 130
   c. 130 – 23 =

Uh oh! I lost Calculator.

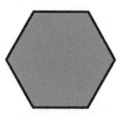

1. How many lines of symmetry does this figure have?

2. Heathrow Airport in London, England employs 80 chefs to prepare meals for international flights. The cooks produce 160,000 meals each week. If they share the work evenly, how many meals does each chef prepare?

3. Use mental math to solve.

   Five times nine minus six =

4. Someone spins this spinner once. What are the chances that the result will be purple?

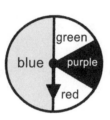

5. Owen will use the scale to enlarge the jumbo jet to make a poster for his bedroom. How long will the jet in his poster be?

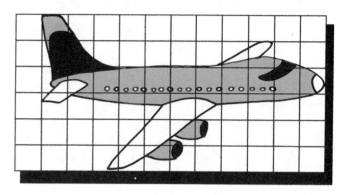

Scale: side of each square = 4 cm

---

1. Solve the problem.   **25 x 64 =**

2. Every day 3,000,000 people travel by air. Ten percent of the travelers land somewhere in France. How many people land in France each day? *(Hint: To find the percent of a number, change the percent to a decimal and multiply.)*

3. Round each decimal to the nearest whole number.

   a. 43.24   b. 57.6   c. 120.8

4. Which equation is solved accurately?

   a. y + 19 = 31   b. p − 4 = 32
        y = 12   p = 28
            c. n + 11 = 31
                n = 31

We fly everywhere.

5. Shannon drank two 12-ounce cans of soda pop during her cross-country flight. Fill in the blanks with the terms below that will make the statement true.

   more than   less than   equal to

   Shannon drank

   _____ **a quart**

   and _____ **a pint**

   of soda on her flight.

1. Bethany bought the following items to carry in her backpack on her flight. Estimate the sum of her purchases. _____

2. Calculate the actual sum. _____

3. She gave the clerk fifteen dollars. What change did she receive?

    _____

paperback.....$5.95
bottled water.....$1.64
peanuts.....$1.65
batteries iPod.....$2.75

4. She decided to spend her change on a sports magazine that cost $3.50. Since she didn't have enough money for the magazine, she asked her dad to lend her just enough to be able to get it. How much money did she borrow?

    _____

5. Challenge Problem

The world is divided into 24 time zones. This map shows the six time zones for the U. S. Notice that the time is later in the east than the west at any point during the day. Complete the table below to show the arrival time for each flight, taking into consideration the fact that you may be traveling to a different time zone.

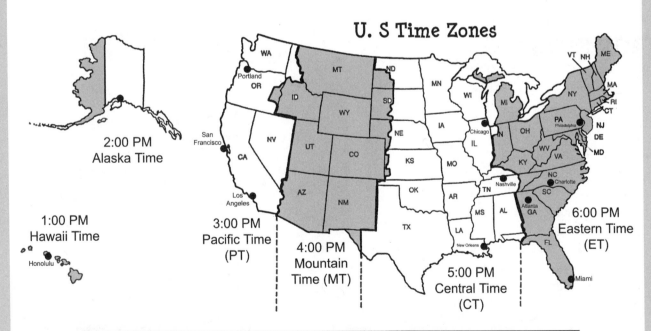

U. S Time Zones

2:00 PM
Alaska Time

1:00 PM
Hawaii Time

3:00 PM
Pacific Time
(PT)

4:00 PM
Mountain
Time (MT)

5:00 PM
Central Time
(CT)

6:00 PM
Eastern Time
(ET)

Depart From	Destination	Travel Time	Departure Time	Arrival Time
Chicago, IL	San Francisco, CA	3H 42 Min	9:26 am	
Portland, OR	New Orleans, LA	4H 6 Min	12:11 pm	
Nashville, TN	Philadelphia, PA	1H 21 Min	7:33 am	
Charlotte, NC	Atlanta, GA	1 H	1:56 pm	
Miami, FL	Los Angeles, CA	4 H 41 Min	3:42 pm	
Los Angeles, CA	Honolulu, HI	5 H 7 Min	8:58 am	

1. Megan was able to attend swimming practice only on Monday, Tuesday, and Friday. How many hours of practice did she miss?

SWIM TEAM PRACTICE SCHEDULE

M	T	W	Th	F
2:45 – 4:30pm	3:15 – 4:15pm	2:45 – 4:30pm	3:15 – 4:15pm	4:00 – 5:30pm

2. Use the distributive property to solve.

$3 \times (6 + 4) = (3 \times 6) + (3 \times 4) =$ _____

3. Find the surface area of a cube that has 4-cm sides.

4. These figures are *(circle one)*:

similar   symmetrical   congruent   typical

5. Use the bar graph to answer these:

a. Which country won one more gold medal than Germany?

b. Which two countries won the same number of gold medals?

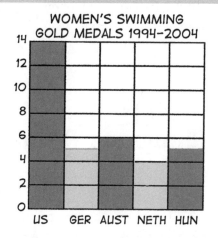

WOMEN'S SWIMMING GOLD MEDALS 1994–2004

US GER AUST NETH HUN

---

1. Several world-class swimmers have attempted to swim the English Channel between France and Great Britain (570 km long). Since even the best swimmers can swim only about eight kilometers per hour, about how many hours would you expect it to take an expert swimmer to swim the channel?

2. Find 40% of 16.

3. Peter and Pam are both avid swimmers. Last week Pete swam twice as many hours as Pam. Together they swam a total 18 hours. How many hours did each swim?

4. Use a protractor to measure the angles.

Angle A = _____   Angle B = _____   Angle C = _____

5. Finish the function table with this rule:

S = P – 2

S	P
	7
3	
	8
9	
	12

WEDNESDAY WEEK 8 _____ MATH PRACTICE
Name

1. How many faces are on this figure?

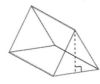

2. Which unit of measurement would be most appropriate for finding the capacity of a swimming pool?

   a. gallons   b. quarts   c. pounds   d. pints

3. Add the correct operational signs to make a true statement.

(16 ☐ 3) ☐ 4 = 12

4. Find the mode for the list of numerals.

17   18   12   18   22   16   18   17

5. Find the circumference of the pool deck to determine the number of meters of safety fencing needed.
(Hint: Circumference = diameter x 3.14.)

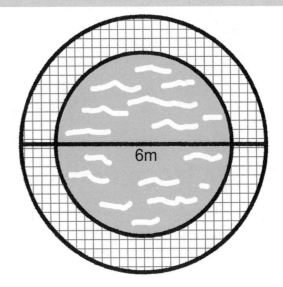

6m

THURSDAY WEEK 8 _____ MATH PRACTICE
Name

1. A raft has a capacity of 75 pounds. Should two ten-year old boys float on this raft at the same time? Tell why or why not.

2. Simplify the expression. Then find the answer if p = 6.

$9p - 4p =$ $p =$

3. Draw on or above the number line to solve.

$3 + {-}6 =$ _____

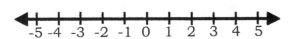

4. Decide if each fraction is closer to $\frac{1}{2}$ or 1 whole. Write H or W beneath each one.

$\frac{1}{3}$ $\frac{3}{5}$ $\frac{7}{8}$ $\frac{11}{12}$ $\frac{3}{8}$ $\frac{5}{6}$

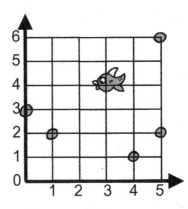

5. a. The fish is located at point (3, 4). Write the coordinates for each of the bubbles. _____ , _____ ,
_____ , _____ , _____

   b. Draw another bubble somewhere on the graph. Write its coordinates:
_____

1. Kacie swam for 12 hours this week at the YMCA pool. 25% of her pool time was spent on free swim. The rest was in swimming classes. How many hours did Kacie spend in swimming classes?

2. Solve the problem. Write the answer in lowest terms.

$$2\frac{3}{5} + 3\frac{4}{5} =$$

3. Diana Nyad, a world class swimmer, battled fatigue, jellyfish and strong currents as she swam the 60 miles from the Bahamas to Florida. It took her $27\frac{1}{2}$ hours to complete her journey. *About* how many miles did she swim each hour?

4. Complete the multiples chart. Then circle the multiples that **3** and **4** have in common.

X	1	2	3	4	5	6	7	8	9	10	11	12
3	3	6	9									
4	4	8	12									

5. Challenge Problem

Hidden Valley Motel has built a new swimming pool that is 32 feet long and 24 feet wide. The owners have hired a tiling expert to lay a 4-foot wide tile deck around the entire pool.

a. Draw a diagram of the pool and deck on the grid. Label the measurements of the pool.

b. Think! What are **two** ways to find the area of the deck?

_____

_____

_____

_____

_____

c. Each bundle of tiles covers 24 square feet and costs $49.95. How many bundles of tiles will the motel owners need to purchase for their project?

_____

d. What is the total cost of the tiles?

_____

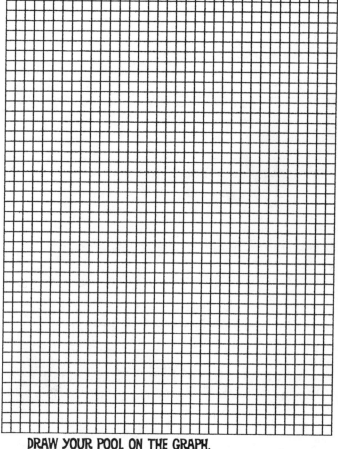

DRAW YOUR POOL ON THE GRAPH.

MONDAY WEEK 9 — Bianca Anton

Name

MATH PRACTICE

1. When trying to finish an invention, Thomas Edison sometimes worked for 72 hours without stopping. How many days is that? $3\frac{1}{2}$

   $\begin{array}{r} 24 \\ \times\ 3 \\ \hline 62 \\ +24 \\ \hline 86 \end{array}$

2. Solve the problem. **8.23 x 2.3 =** 41.15

3. Choose the appropriate unit to measure the capacity of each container—liter or milliliter. (Write *l* or *ml*.)

   _l_ a. wading pool   _ml_ d. soup spoon

   _ml_ b. mug   _l_ e. bath tub

   _l_ c. aquarium

4. Ten face-down letter cards spell the word "phonograph," one of Thomas Edison's most famous inventions. If you draw one, what is the chance of drawing:

   a. a vowel? _3%_

   b. a letter of the alphabet? _10%_

5. Draw a line of symmetry on the light bulb.

What a bright idea.

$\begin{array}{r} 8.23 \\ \times\ 2.3 \\ \hline 24.69 \\ +16.46 \\ \hline 41.15 \end{array}$

TUESDAY WEEK 9 — Bianca Anton

Name

MATH PRACTICE

1. Twenty-four students from Edison Elementary School in West Orange, New Jersey took a field trip to the nearby Edison National Historic Site. Each student paid $6.50 to cover the cost of admission and transportation. How much money was collected? $39.00

   $\begin{array}{r} 6.50 \\ \times\ 24 \\ \hline 26.00 \\ +13.00 \\ \hline 39.00 \end{array}$

2. Solve the problem.

   $\begin{array}{r} \overset{2}{3}\text{ feet }\overset{14}{2}\text{ inches} \\ -\ 1\text{ foot }9\text{ inches} \\ \hline 1\text{ foot }5\text{ inches} \end{array}$

3. Write this numeral in standard form.

   twenty-four thousand six hundred ninety seven   (24,697)

4. Substitute the value of each letter to solve the equation.

   LETTER VALUES

   G = 0   H = 4   I = 3
   L = 2   T = 5

   ## L + I + G + H + T 23045

5. Fill in the missing values on the table. Explain how the exponent affects the number of zeros in each answer.

EXPONENT FORM	STANDARD FORM
10^1	10
10^2	100
10^3	
10^4	
10^5	

   I know this.

1. Multiply 11×10^2 to learn how many invention patents Tom Edison acquired in his lifetime.

2. Solve the problem.   **(12 + 24) ÷ 3 =**

3. Read the weights on the books pictured below (# 4). How much do the four books weigh in all? _____ pounds, _____ ounces

4. Jose wants to check out two of the invention books. What are the possible combinations of books he could choose?

14 oz. — Thomas Edison, Boy Inventor
12 oz. — 100 POPULAR INVENTIONS
8 oz. — BE AN INVENTOR
15 oz. — THE AGE OF INVENTIONS

5. Draw a line to match each quadrilateral with its name. (Some may have more than one name.)

A   **square**

B   **rectangle**

C   **rhombus**

D   **parallelogram**

1. Thomas Edison spent $125,000 per year for eight years on his invention of the storage battery. How much did he spend in all?

2. At 6:00 a.m. on July 1, the temperature was a pleasant 68°F. By 2:00 p.m. it was 94°F. How much did the temperature rise?

3. A dedicated scientist devoted 5 hours and 15 minutes each day to his new invention. At that rate, how many hours and minutes did he work in nine days?

4. 45% of the 40 volunteers at the Thomas Edison Historical Site are senior citizens. How many assistants are seniors? *(Formula: Change % to a decimal and multiply.)*

5. What is the value of y for each of the following equations?

$$31 - y = 14$$

$$y + 43 = 60$$

$$y - 12 = 5$$

a. y = 15

b. y = 16

c. y = 17

I think I know this.

I almost forgot my umbrella.

1. What are the next two numbers?

1, 2, 6, 24, _____ , _____

2. Add the correct symbol (**<, >,** or **=**) to make the statement true.

7 + (6 x 4) ☐ **(8 x 4)**

3. If a circle's diameter is 18 cm, its radius is _____.

4. Circle **all** of the fractions that are equivalent to $\frac{3}{5}$.

$\frac{6}{10}, \frac{12}{15}, \frac{9}{15}, \frac{15}{25}$

5. Challenge Problem

Solve the following equations to learn facts about Thomas Edison. Then write the letter that follows each fact in the blank above the number that matches each answer.

a. When he was ($\frac{1}{8}$ of 64) or ___ years old, his mom, a schoolteacher, decided to teach him at home. **T**

b. Tom took his first job as a newsboy on The Grand Trunk Railroad when he was (18 x 2) ÷ 3 or ____ years old. **N**

c. The first power station, built by Edison, supplied power for 2 x 102 or ____ lamps. **A**

d. Edison's telephone system connected New York and Philadelphia, a total of 172,000 meters or ___ kilometers. **U**

e. The first motion picture studio, built by Tom Edison, was 1,520 centimeters or ___ meters long. **S**

f. The first public viewing in Edison's motion picture studio occurred in the year 1958 – 65 or _____. **W**

g. Edison lost ($\frac{1}{5}$ of $25,000,000) or _____ when his laboratories burned in West Orange, New Jersey. **G**

h. Edison employed (50 x 40) or _____ workers to help him with his experiments. **A**

i. Edison worked on developing a goldenrod plant that was 156 inches or _____ feet tall because it contained rubber that was useful for many products. **I**

j. Thomas Edison was most productive for (882 ÷ 42), a period of ___ years when he was between the ages of 32 and 53. This time is known as "The Age of Edison." **E**

k. Edison lived for (116 – 32) or _____ years. **H**

Find the letter that goes with each answer to find a remark made about Tom Edison.

___ ___ ___ ___ ___ ___ ___ ___ ___ ___ ___
1,893   84   2,000   8   240   5,000,000   21   12   13   172   15.2

1. Niagara Falls, on New York-Canadian border, is one of the world's largest waterfalls. The Canadian Falls is 670 meters wide while the American Falls measures 328 meters. Which operation would you use to compare the sizes of the two falls?

    a. addition   c. multiplication

    b. subtraction   d. division

2. Solve the problem.   **57 + 19.8 =**

3. Match each picture with the correct name.

    line segment   ray   line

4. The National Park Service at Niagara Falls wants to make a graph comparing the number of tourists who visit the falls each season in a particular year. Which graph would best communicate the information?

    a. line graph   b. pie graph   c. bar graph

Wheeee!

5. Use the scale to estimate the height of Horseshoe Falls.

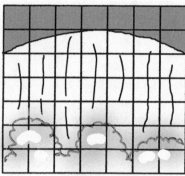

Scale: side of each square = 28 ft

1. Write an equation that matches the statement.

    Subtract a number from 45 and the result will be 18.

2. Write the number in expanded form.

    162,361 =

    _____ + _____ + ____ + ____ + ____ + ___

3. Is this answer correct?

    13 – 6.4 = 6.6

4. Henry and Jen Kelley, an elderly couple, visited Niagara Falls every other winter during their 62-year marriage. How many times did they enjoy the falls?

5. How many cubic feet would it take to fill a cubic yard?

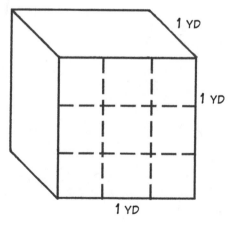
1 YD
1 YD
1 YD

WEDNESDAY WEEK 10 _____ MATH PRACTICE

1. The Niagara Falls gift shop kept a record of the number of post cards sold over 7 days. What was the mean number sold per day?

S	M	T	W	TH	F	S
450	275	0	300	350	480	575

2. Choose the example of the identity property of addition.

○ (a + b) + c = a + (b + c)   ○ a + b = b + a
○ a + b = b − a   ○ a + 0 = a

3. Use mental math to solve.

A French explorer saw the falls in 1613. Sixty-five years later a Belgian priest explored the area. What year did the priest see the falls?

4. Estimate the length of segment ST to the nearest half inch. Then use a ruler to check your guess.

Estimate: ____ inches   Actual: ____ inches

S _____ T

5. Match each figure below with the correct description.

a. A right triangle has a 90-degree angle.

b. All of the sides in a scalene triangle have different lengths.

c. All the sides and all the angles of an equilateral triangle have the same measurement.

d. Two sides and two angles of an isosceles triangle have the same measurement.

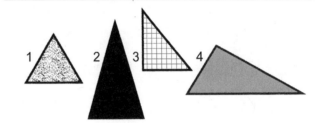

THURSDAY WEEK 10 _____ MATH PRACTICE

1. Write the numeral for **five hundred seventy-six and three tenths**.

2. Is the answer correct if p = 12?

$$2p + 4 = 24$$

3. Erosion at Niagara Falls was once such a serious problem that the water's edge was receding (being pushed back) three feet each year. At that rate, how many years would it have taken for Niagara Falls to recede 120 feet?

4. Solve the problem. $3.5\overline{)4.62}$

5. Which angle is most like the angle of the American Falls?

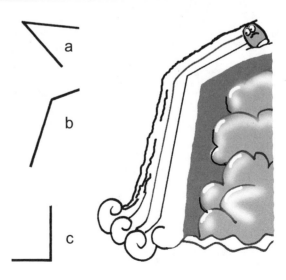

1. The average amount of water that goes over the falls each second is equal to one hundred ninety four thousand, nine hundred forty cubic feet. Write that numeral in standard notation.

2. Which operation sign makes the answer correct? **(27 ☐ 12) x 3 = 45**

3. Thirty-five out of every 100 tourists at Niagara Falls in June came from a foreign country. Write this information as:

    a. a fraction _____   b. a decimal _____   c. a percent _____

4. Use the illustration to solve the problem.

We're going over the falls in tandem.

$$5 \div \frac{1}{2} = \underline{\quad}$$

5. Challenge Problem

The Monroe family (Mom, Dad, 11-year old Keri, and 3-year old Sam) wants to make the most of their day in Niagara Falls while using their money wisely. Help them decide which tour offers the most economical way to experience Niagara Falls. Notice that with Misty Falls Tours they can pay for each attraction separately. The All Season Tours company charges one price for all events.

Misty Falls Tours

Tour	Adults	Kids 5-12
Maid of the Mist Boat Ride	$31.95	$18.95
Skylon Tower Tour	$12.95	$6.95
Niagara Park Carriage Ride	$4.50	$2.95
Buffet Lunch	$11.95	$7.95

(Kids under five - Free)

All Seasons Tours

Purchase a package tour and take in all of the following:

Maid of the Mist Boat Ride, a tour of Skylon Tower, a carriage ride through Niagara Park, and a buffet lunch at the Niagara Inn.

Adults..........$65.90
Kids 5-12:....$41.00
Under 5:.......Free

    a. Find the total family cost of a Misty Falls experience.

    b. Find the cost for the family with All Seasons Tours.

    c. Tell which touring company is most economical for the Monroes.

    d. Calculate the savings with the best plan.

1. Circle the bikes that are similar.

2. Circle the information that is missing from the problem but is needed to solve it.

15% of the bikes on the playground are red. How many red bikes in all?

   a. 30 bikes are black.

   b. There are 42 road bikes and a few mountain bikes in the rack.

   c. The bike rack is $\frac{2}{3}$ full.

   d. There are 80 bikes in the bike rack.

3. Solve the problem.
349 x 18=

4. Find the area.

12 m
15 m
6 m
12 m

5. Ramon is buying a new bike and has narrowed his choices to a green road bike or a black mountain bike. He has the option of adding a light, a mirror or both to either bike. Draw a tree diagram that shows the possible bikes with extras Ramon could purchase.

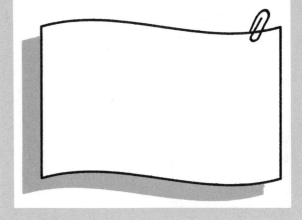

1. Notice the factors and common factors for 12 and 15. Fill in the second chart with the factors for 16 and 20. Circle the common factor(s).

12	15		16	20
4x3	5x3			
6x2	15x1			
12x1				

2. Emily returned from her morning bike ride at 11:43 a.m. after a one hour and 30 minute ride. What time did she start riding?

3. Estimate the sum.

   986 + 222 + 49 + 18 =

4. In 1993 four men rode their bikes from the northern tip of Africa to the southern tip. During the 260 days of the trip they rode close to 12,000 miles. Use a *calculator* to find out how many miles they averaged each day. Round to the nearest whole number.

5. a. Complete the function table.

   b. What pattern do you notice on the **Input** side of the table?

I love function tables.

INPUT	OUTPUT
59	
54	
49	
44	
39	
34	

OUTPUT = INPUT − 3

1. a. Use the formula to find the circumference for each of the bike wheels.

(C = d x 3.14)

b. Find the difference between the two wheels.

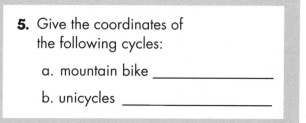

2. Two students solved the problem. Who's correct?

$$5 + (8 \times 7) - 2 =$$

___ Marna's answer = 59

___ Josh's answer = 89

3. Lance Armstrong was born in Plano, Texas in 1971. How old was he when he won

    a. his first Tour de France in 1999? _____

    b. his sixth Tour de France in 2005? _____

4. Draw a parallelogram.

5. Give the coordinates of the following cycles:

    a. mountain bike _____

    b. unicycles _____

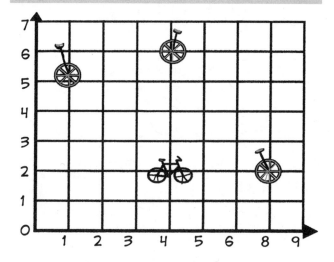

1. Write the correct symbol (**<** , **>**, or **=**) in the space.

$$\frac{6}{8} \ \square \ \frac{3}{4}$$

2. The Forever Bicycle Factory in Shanghai, China makes 4,500 bikes every day. At this rate, how many bikes are made in the month of April?

3. Simplify the equation. Then solve with $s = 16$.

$$2s + 3s - s =$$

4. Solve the problem using mental math.

$$30,000 \div 10 =$$

5. The highlighted angle in the bicycle wheel is

    a. a right angle

    b. an acute angle

    c. an obtuse angle

Name

1. Solve the problem.

$$3 - 1\frac{1}{8} =$$

2. 85% of the 16,000,000 people in the Netherlands own a bike, and most of them ride every day! Which equation would you use to find how many people own bikes in Netherlands?

    a. 16,000,000 − 85 =   b. 0.85 x 16,000,000 =   c. 16,000 x 85% =   d. not here

3. Which of the equivalent fractions is in lowest terms?

    a. $\frac{3}{4}$ b. $\frac{6}{8}$

4. Jeanie Longo, of France, holds the women's distance record for riding 28 miles in one hour on December 7, 2000. At that rate how many miles could Jeanie ride between 9:00 a.m. and noon?

5. Challenge Problem

The Wonder Wheels Bike Club had their annual leisurely one-mile ride and picnic at Crystal Pond Park. Folks of all ages and sizes showed up with unicycles, tricycles, and bicycles. A bystander counted 83 wheels as he watched the cycles ride around the pond. What combination of bikes, trikes, and unicycles **might** have been at the event?

Solve the problem in two different ways.

Solution One: _____ tricycles

               _____ bicycles

               _____ unicycles

Solution Two: _____ tricycles

               _____ bicycles

               _____ unicycles

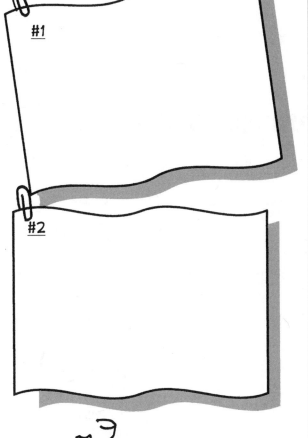

#1

#2

1. Temperatures at the North Pole drop as low as –40°F in the winter and rise as high as 32°F in the summer. What is the range between the lowest and highest North Pole temperatures?

2. Use the number line to solve. **–5 + 12 =**

3. Explorer Robert Peary and his crew used sleds and dogs on many expeditions to the North Pole. Conditions were so harsh that the group could travel only 30 miles per day. How many kilometers is this? *(Hint: 1 mile = 1.62 kilometers.)*

4. Which space figure does the igloo most closely resemble?

   a. sphere   c. hemisphere

   b. curve   d. circle

5. How many students want to study in Australia?

FAVORITE REGIONS TO STUDY	
SURVEY OF 94 MIDDLE SCHOOL STUDENTS	
15	NORTH POLE
7	ANTARCTICA
12	SOUTH AMERICA
19	EUROPE
13	ASIA
	AUSTRALIA
7	AFRICA
19	NORTH AMERICA

1. Write the numeral named by the words below.

thirty five and six hundredths

2. Pure water freezes at 32 degrees Fahrenheit. Sea water, because of its salt, freezes at 28.4°F. How many degrees does the water temperature have to drop before freezing . . .

   a. in Lake Erie when the temperature is 41°F? _____

   b. in the Indian Ocean when the temperature is 30.2°F?
_____

3. Which operation makes this equation correct?

$$(13 \ \boxed{} \ 4) \times 5 + 9 = 54$$

   a. addition   c. multiplication

   b. subtraction   d. division

4. Complete Problem #5. Then assume that the portion of the iceberg shown above the surface weighs 10 tons. About how much would the underwater part weigh?

5. If the iceberg extends 30 feet above the water, how far below the water does it extend?

38

WEDNESDAY WEEK 12 _____ MATH PRACTICE

Name

1. Estimate the number of degrees in the pictured angle.

    a. 45   b. 150   c. 110   d. 80

2. The average depth of the Arctic Ocean is 1300 meters. About how many feet deep is the Arctic Ocean? *(Hint: A meter is a little more than 3 feet.)*

    a. 4000   c. 1300

    b. 13,000   d. none of these

3. Solve the problem.

$$\frac{2}{6} + \frac{1}{4} =$$

4. Find the median number in the list.

    14 20 18 26 10 22 8 6 16

5. Robert Peary's expedition got credit for reaching the North Pole first in 1909. Forty-nine years later the United States submarine *Nautilus* became the first vessel to pass under the ice at the North Pole.

    a. When did the *Nautilus* accomplish its underwater feat?

    b. How many years ago did this feat take place?

ANS! 1958

A

THURSDAY WEEK 12 _____ MATH PRACTICE

Name

1. Solve the problem.

    4 + (18 x 2) + (9 ÷ 3) =

2. In the 1800s, dog sleds weighed 150 kilograms, while modern-day sleds weigh 30 kilograms. Write a ratio that compares the weight of an 1800s sled to a modern-day one.

3. Turn the exponential number into a standard numeral and solve the problem.

    $63 \times 10^3 =$

4. Which is an example of the commutative property of multiplication?

    a. (r x s) = r x s   c. r + 1 = r

    b. r + s = s + r   d. r x s = s x r

5. If each of the dogs in Robert Peary's eight-dog team pulled equally, how many kilograms of weight would each dog pull?

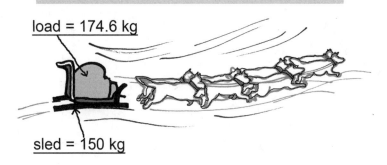

load = 174.6 kg

sled = 150 kg

1. Solve the problem. **23.5 + 0.08 + 5.3 =**

2. Check for accuracy.

$$39.42$$
$$-18.63$$
$$20.89$$

Coming Soon

THE ADVENTURE MOVIE HIT OF THE SEASON

ARCTIC JOURNEY
Robert Perry's
North Pole Adventure

Adults.....$5.95
13-18......$3.95
9-12........$2.95

*Content not appropriate
for children under nine.*

3. The polar ice cap is about 30 feet deep. How many yards deep is the ice cap?

4. Find the admission cost for two adults, two teenagers, and one ten-year old to see the movie.

5. Challenge Problem

Some middle grades students who studied the North Pole learned that the decade of the 1980s was a busy one for expeditions to the pole, with six teams successfully making the overland trek. The class decided to create a mind teaser with the information they learned. Read the clues about the team leaders of these expeditions. Then list each leader's name and year of arrival on the Expedition Chart, in the order in which they reached the North Pole.

a. The last two digits of Helen Thayer's arrival year are the same. 1988

b. Will Steger and Jean-Louis Etienne arrived the same year and the only year that had two successful expeditions. 1976

c. Fukashi Kazami arrived one year after Jean-Louis Etienne and two years before Robert Swan.

d. The last two digits of Sir Ranulph Fiennes' arrival year add up to ten. 1982

e. Will Steger arrived ten days before Jean-Louis Etienne.

f. Sir Ranulph Fiennes beat Fukashi Kazami by five years. 1987

g. Robert Swan arrived in an odd-numbered year. 1979

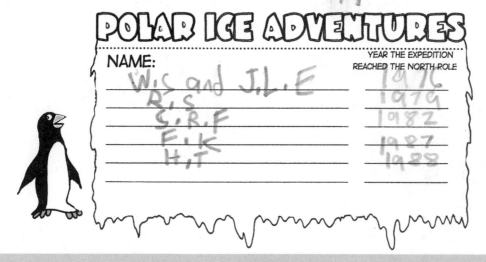

POLAR ICE ADVENTURES

NAME:	YEAR THE EXPEDITION REACHED THE NORTH POLE
W.S and J.L.E	1976
R.S	1979
S.R.F	1982
F.K	1987
H.T	1988

1. Solve the problem by subtracting. Check by adding backwards.

$$3,020 \\ -1,246$$

2. The whale shark, the largest fish in the world, can weigh 15 tons — twice as much as an African elephant! Use the formula to tell how many pounds a whale shark can weigh.
(Hint: 1 ton = 2,000 pounds.)

3. a. Write the next numeral in the series.

   3   33   333   3,333   _____

   b. Write that same number again using words.

   _____

4. Fill in the blanks.

   Scott's aquarium has _____ faces,

   _____ vertices, and _____ edges.

5. Of the 360 known species of sharks, only 20% of them will grow longer than 2 meters. Show this information on the pie graph according to the key.

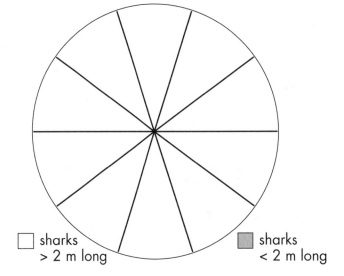

☐ sharks
> 2 m long

▨ sharks
< 2 m long

1. Find the equation that matches the statement.

   "I'm thinking of a number. If I divide it by 3 and subtract 2, the answer will be 3."

   a. $x + 2 \div 3 = 3$ c. $(9 \times 2) + x = 3$

   b. $(x \div 3) - 2 = 3$ d. None of these

2. Mako sharks can swim up to 48 kilometers per hour. Estimate the distance a Mako shark can travel if it swims steadily for one hour and 30 minutes.

3. Round each number to the nearest whole number and estimate the sum.

   $9.31 + 4.8 + 6.03 =$

4. Marty bought the poster (in problem #5) for $6.75. He gave the salesperson a ten-dollar bill. How much was his change?

5. Find the area of the poster.

36 in

18 in

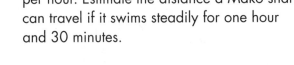

Use It! Don't Lose It! IP 613-0

1. Ten beans are lying on a table. Each bean has one different number, 1–10. If you choose a bean with your eyes closed, what is the chance of choosing a prime number?

2. Is this answer correct? $\frac{3}{5} + \frac{3}{5} + \frac{2}{5} = 1\frac{2}{5}$

3. The body temperature of most sharks matches the temperature of the water they live in. However, blue sharks and Mako sharks can raise their temperature 18 degrees above the water temperature when they swim fast. What is the water temperature if the fast-moving blue shark's temperature is 92 degrees Fahrenheit?

4. Which figure is congruent to the first one?

       a   b   c   d

5. Find the average length of a pygmy shark.

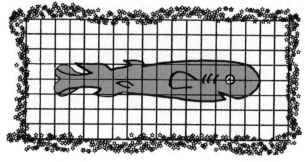

Scale: sides of squares $= \frac{1}{2}''$

He looks small on paper.

1. Solve the problem. $\frac{3}{4} + \frac{2}{3} =$

2. Find p if $s = 7$ **$p + s = 16$**

   a. 9   b. 12   c. 6   d. 7

3. Half of all sharks grow to be 40 inches or longer. Of the 360 different kinds of sharks, how many kinds are less than 40 inches long?

4. Solve the problem.

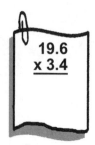
```
19.6
x 3.4
```

Swim for your life!

5. Sharks have keen vision. In clear water they can spot their prey from 70 feet away. What other measurement unit reasonably could be used to tell the distance between the shark and its prey?

   a. inches

   b. kilometers

   c. meters

   d. miles

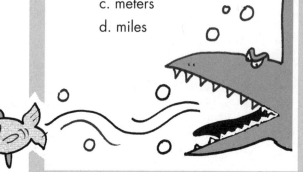

1. What was the average number of sightings for each of the four months? _____

2. Write a lowest terms fraction to compare the number of sightings in May with the number in June. _____

3. How many more sightings occurred in August than in May? _____

4. Twenty-five percent of the sharks sighted in August were less than one meter long. How many were under a meter? _____

Caribbean Sea Shark Sightings

Month	Number
May	卌 IIII
June	卌 卌 卌 III
July	卌 卌 I
August	卌 卌 卌 卌 IIII

5. Challenge Problem

What information is still needed to solve each real life problem? (Some is missing!)

a. In 2000 there were 79 reported shark attacks around the world. What's the difference in the number of attacks between 2002 and 2000?

_____

b. Shark fin soup, a delicacy is Asia, is sold for $90.00 a bowl. How much money did Chung's Seafood Restaurant make on shark fin soup last Saturday night?

_____

c. The number of sharks has dropped by 40% in the last 15 years. What was the shark population 15 years ago?

_____

d. The smallest sharks weigh only 1 ounce. How many ounces does the whole school weigh?

_____

e. The young nurse shark will grow to be four feet long. How many feet and inches will it grow before it reaches its full size?

_____

f. The lemon shark's lost tooth will grow back in only eight days. How many more days before the lost tooth is back?

_____

1. a. The book is _____ cm tall and _____ cm wide.

    b. The area of the book's cover is _____ square centimeters.

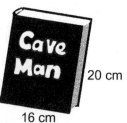

20 cm

16 cm

2. The sum of two consecutive numbers is 47. The product is 552. What are the numbers? *(Hint: Consecutive numbers are side by side numbers such as 2 and 3, or 14 and 15.)*

3. Solve the problem.

1,243
x 68

4. Draw a line of symmetry in the longest stalactite.

5. What is the mean length of the three longest caves in Europe?

Longest European Caves

Name	Country	Length
Siebenhengste Cave...	*Switzerland* ...	149 k
Holloch....................	*Switzerland* ...	189 k
Optimisticeskaja.........	*Ukraine*	214 k

1. Which sign makes the equation correct?

$$3 + 9 + (4 \;\square\; 8) - 6 = 38$$

    a. +   b. –   c. x   d. ÷

2. Luke got 8 out of 10 answers correct on his quiz about Mammoth Cave. What percentage grade did he receive?

3. Simplify and solve, if r = 11.

$$3r + 2r + 5r - 2r =$$

Go figure!

4. What unit of measurement describes the volume of a pitcher that holds enough juice to serve a family of four?

    a. liter   b. milliliter   c. ounce   d. pint

5. a. Draw the next three coins to complete the pattern.

    b. Calculate the amount of money: _____

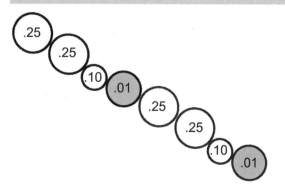

.25   .25   .10   .01   .25   .25   .10   .01

1. Estimate the length in centimeters of segment LM.

 a. 10 cm   b. 3 cm   c. 7 cm   d. 5 cm

 L _____ M

2. Wes Skiles, an experienced SCUBA diver, has made 3,000 dives into underwater caves. Which of the following equations have 3,000 as their product?

 a. 30 x 10 =   c. 60 x 50 =

 b. 300 x 10 =   d. 15 x 20 =

3. Jenna is deciding on the outfit she'll wear for a caving adventure. She will choose either blue jeans or black jeans, and one shirt: yellow, green, or red. How many different possibilities does she have?

4. Draw a pair of perpendicular lines.

5. Which statement can you determine is true from the information shown?

 a. Mammoth Cave is longer than the length of the other caves combined.

 b. Mammoth Cave is more than three times the length of Jewel Cave.

 c. Mammoth Cave is the longest cave in the world.

 d. The lengths of Wind Cave, Fisher Ridge, and Lechugilla Caves can all be accurately rounded to 110 miles.

Longest U.S. Caves

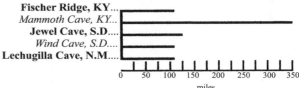

Fischer Ridge, KY....
Mammoth Cave, KY...
Jewel Cave, S.D....
Wind Cave, S.D....
Lechugilla Cave, N.M....

0   50   100   150   200   250   300   350
miles

1. It took Sheck Exley, who set many world underwater diving records, 23 minutes to dive 867 feet into Mexico's Nacimiento Cave. Use division to find how many feet he traveled each minute. (Round to the nearest foot.)

2. Find m if n = 25   **n + m = 53**

3. The diameter of a cave's mouth is 28 inches. Use the formula to find the circumference.

 (Circumference = 3.14 x diameter)

4. Solve the equation to find how many miles of passage are contained in the Mammoth Cave in Kentucky.
(Hint: Follow the order of operation PEAS— parentheses, exponents, addition, subtraction.)

 3^3 + (60 x 5) + 28 − 3 =

5. The sum of the outer dominoes is 11. Which domino could be added to an end to change the outer sum to a multiple of 5?

 _____

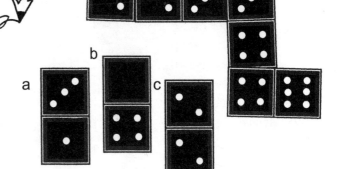

a   b   c

Solve 1–4 to find the correct date for the event. Write the number of each event (1–4) on the timeline.

Timeline of Caving Discoveries and Events

A.D. 1840 1850 1860 1870 1880 1890 1890 1900 1910 1920 1930 1940 1950 1960 1970 1980 1990 2000 2010

1. Jewel Cave was discovered in South Dakota 100 years before the beginning of the 21st century.

2. Mammoth Cave became a National Park in

$$10^3 + (1,000 - 100) + (8 \times 5) + 1 =$$

3. Ancient cave art was discovered in France in

$$1,000 + 900 + 90 + 4 =$$

4. Lechuguilla Cave was discovered in New Mexico in the year

$$(50 \times 40) - 14 =$$

5. Challenge Problem

As the discoverer and explorer of a new cave you are responsible for mapping the cave's tunnel. Here's what to do:

a. Cut a 22-centimeter length of string.

b. Lay the string on the grid to mark a path through the cave. The path must begin at the point marked *Entrance* and end at the point marked *Exit*. The rest of the pathway is up to you!

c. On a *separate* sheet of paper, list the sets of coordinates which tell the location of the string on the grid as the path winds its way between the entrance and exit. Don't make any permanent marks on the grid. The first point on the grid after the entrance is point a. List the coordinates for it. The second point is point b. List its coordinates. Continue in this way until your path ends at the cave's exit.

d. Give your cave a name.

e. Remove the string.

f. Trade your grid and list of coordinates with a partner and use the sets of coordinates to determine the path through the cave.

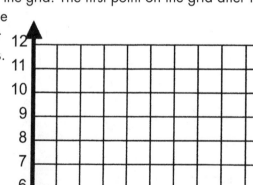

I'm a spelunker.

1. Spanish explorers visited the Amazon rain forest in 1541. President Teddy Roosevelt explored the area in 1914. Which equation will find the number of years between these events?

    a. 1914 + 1541 =   c. x + 1541 = 1914

    b. 1914 – 1541 =   d. answer not here

2. What quadrilateral has all right angles, equal opposite sides, but does not have all equal sides?

3. Which shows the property of one for multiplication?

    a. (a + 1) = (1 + a)   c. a x 1 = a

    b. (a x 1) = (1 x a)   d. a + b = 1

4. About 5 % of the world's rain forests are protected in national parks. What type of graph would be best to compare the amount of protected to unprotected rain forest?

    a. pie graph   c. line graph

    b. coordinate graph   d. none of these

5. Estimate the number of degrees in the angle formed by the branches of the Kapok tree.

    a. 90   c. 45

    b. 75   d. 180

1. Solve. Use the diagram to prove your accuracy.

$$1\frac{2}{5} - \frac{4}{5} =$$

2. Add <, >, or = in each blank to complete the statement. Be sure to work from left to right.

    3.12 ☐ **3.6** ☐ **3.06**

3. In the early 1990s, seventy acres of the rain forest were destroyed every minute. At that rate, how many acres were destroyed in

    a. an hour _____?

    b. a day _____?

4. Complete the function table for the given rule.

Let me calculate that.

Input	Output
3	
7	
2	
1	

Output = Input – 5

5. Use the Celsius thermometer to estimate the range between the average high and low rain forest temperatures.

_____

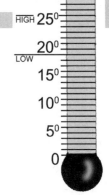

WEDNESDAY WEEK 15 _____ MATH PRACTICE
Name

1. Use mental math to solve.

Half of the world's rain forests are in the area around the Amazon River. If the Amazon rain forest is 1,400,000 square miles, how many square miles of rain forest exist in the world?

2. Solve the problem.

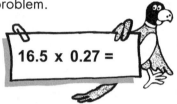

16.5 x 0.27 =

3. The giant trees of the rain forest can grow to 230 feet high. Calculate their height in yards. Round your answer to the nearest whole number.

4. Draw a trapezoid.

5. Someone gives one spin to this spinner. What are the chances that the arrow will land on yellow? Write your answer as a "lowest terms" fraction.

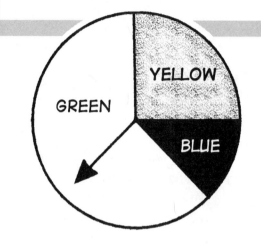

THURSDAY WEEK 15 _____ MATH PRACTICE
Name

1. Write an equation for each of the word phrases.

a. A number (p) minus sixteen equals six

b. Twenty-one plus a number (r) equals twenty-five

2. Shannon began her rain forest report at 4:35 p.m. and worked steadily until supper at 6:15 p.m. How much time has she spent on her report so far? _____

3. Fill in the blank with the correct letter.

The driest places in a rain forest get at least 1.8 meters or _____ centimeters of rain each year!

a. 180

c. 1800

b. 18

d. answer not here

4. Use the number line to solve the problem.

Erin borrowed $5.00 from her mom to buy a rain forest puzzle. She earned $8.50 babysitting. How much will she have after paying back the loan from her mother?

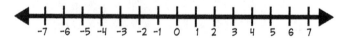

5. Fill in the Venn diagram with the factor(s) of 16 and 12.

1. Write the underlined numeral in exponential form.

   The elevation of a rain forest never exceeds 1,000 meters.

2. One year 65% of the rain forest's 30 feet of rain fell between June and November. How many feet fell in that period of time?
   (Hint: To find the % of a number, change % to a decimal and multiply.)

3. During a cooling trend in the rain forest, the temperature plunged from 76°F to 53°F. How many degrees did the temperature drop?

4. The world's largest flower, the rafflesia, weighs 7 kg, lives in the rain forest, and smells very bad! Use the formula to find how many pounds the flower weighs.
   (Formula: kilograms x 2.2 = pounds)

I love my rainforest home.

5. Challenge

Solve the **Prime Puzzle**. Draw a path from Begin to End that connects only prime numbers or the numeral one and yields a sum of 150. Move either vertically or horizontally to connect numbers.

BEGIN

1	11	15	2	7	9	4	3
3	5	7	3	11	13	12	23
2	7	11	1	5	4	9	7
3	0	17	19	23	8	2	3
5	6	4	15	31	7	11	5
13	11	2	5	7	3	31	4
37	9	3	1	2	7	5	13
11	7	5	6	3	2	16	8
4	3	2	13	5	9	7	15

END

Here's an interesting rainforest fact: the rainforest has 150 kinds of beetles.

1. Draw a figure that is congruent to the one shown.

2. In 1999, four German mechanics took the engine from one Volkswagen Beetle and installed it in another in 97 seconds! How long did this take in minutes and seconds?

3. Solve using mental math.
   a. 169 x 10 =
   b. 169 x 100 =
   c. 169 x 1000 =

4. A racer spins this spinner once to choose the kind of car he'll drive in the race. (H = Honda, C = Chevy, F = Ford.) What is the probability of . . .
   a. spinning Honda? _____
   b. spinning Ford? _____

5. What is the difference between the 1898 record and Henry Seagrave's record? _____

EARLIEST CAR SPEED RECORDS

Driver	Year	Speed (k/hr)
Gaston de Chasseloup-Laubat	1898	63.15
Camille Janatsy	1899	66.66
Louis Rigolly	1904	160
Henry Segrave	1927	322

1. Write each improper fraction as a mixed number. Draw a picture to verify each answer.

   a. $\frac{9}{2}$ = _____   b. $\frac{12}{5}$ = _____

2. How many variables are there in the following expression? ____

   (2 p + q) – m = 19

3. In the expression in problem #2, find the value of *m* if *p* = 8 and *q* = 10.

4. Measure the length of the mini-car to the nearest millimeter.

5. In 2004, thirty-four million cars were produced by the top ten car-producing countries. Twenty-six percent of the cars were made in Japan. How many cars were produced in Japan in 2004? _____

Name

1. The diameter of the Subaru Outback's tire is 26.5 inches. Find the circumference of the tire. _____

2. Round each numeral to its greatest place value and estimate the difference.

1924 – 321 = ____

3. Draw a line of symmetry on the car bumper.

4. The letters are cut apart, shuffled, and placed in a box.

a. What are the chances of choosing a vowel? _____

b. What are the chances of choosing a letter that comes **before** the letter G in the alphabet? _____

5. Kyle, Lane and Quinn all enjoy building model cars. Use the following information to find how many cars each boy built last year.

a. Together the boys completed 21 cars.

b. Kyle built 1 less than twice as many as Lane.

c. Quinn built three more than Kyle.

d. Lane did not build seventeen of the cars.

Kyle built _____ cars

Quinn built _____ cars

Lane built _____ cars

Name

1. Andy Green set the world's fastest car speed record in 1997 when he reached a speed of 1,228 kilometers per hour. Write the speed in expanded form.

2. The answer is 58. What is the problem?

a. $(8 \times 8) - 9 =$ c. $(6 + 9) \times 4 =$

b. $(32 \div 8) + 50 =$ d. $59 - (64 \div 8) + 7 =$

3. Which operation makes the statement true?

$(19 - 3) + 8 \;\boxed{}\; 6 = 4$

a. subtraction   c. multiplication

b. division   d. not here

4. The Quiet Achiever, a car with a roof of solar cells, traveled 4,800 kilometers across Australia in 20 days. If the car traveled the same distance each day, how many kilometers did it cover each day? _____

5. Which description matches the expression?

$3(15 + n)$

a. the product of a number plus fifteen

b. three times the sum of fifteen and a number

c. a number divided by three

1. At 10:00 p.m. the temperature at the Indianapolis Speedway was a chilly 15 degrees Fahrenheit. By 5:00 a.m. it had dropped another 19 degrees. What was the temperature at 5:00 a.m.? _____

2. This figure has

____ triangles and

____ parallelograms.

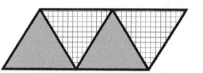

3. The 2000 Honda Accord was advertised at $9,500.00, but Erin's dad purchased it for 10% less. How much did her dad spend for the used Honda? _____

4. Irvin Gordon's 1966 Volvo set a car mileage record for driving 2,219,715 miles over a period of 38 years. What is the value of the numeral 9 in the mileage reading? _____

5. Challenge Problem

a. The approximate distance through the mountains following Corkscrew Curves is

___ 50 miles   ___ 30 miles   ___ 150 miles   ___ 200 miles

b. How long would it take a car racing along the course at 80 mph (miles per hour) to get from Prickly Point Pit Stop through Daring Dune Ridge?

___ less than an hour

___ 1–2 hours

___ more than 2 hours

c. What is the distance on the course from the first time the course crosses the river to the second time it crosses the river?

___ about 100 miles

___ about 200 miles

___ about 300 miles

___ about 50 miles

d. Could a racer averaging 70 mph complete the entire race course in 5 hours? _____

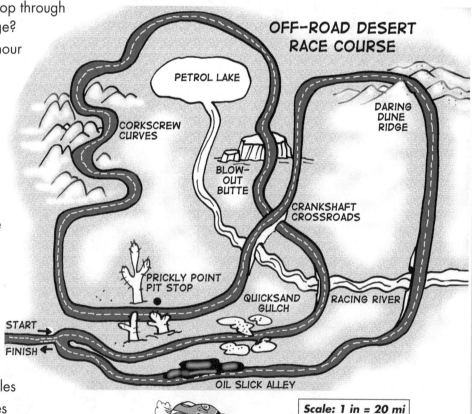

OFF-ROAD DESERT RACE COURSE

PETROL LAKE

CORKSCREW CURVES

DARING DUNE RIDGE

BLOW-OUT BUTTE

CRANKSHAFT CROSSROADS

PRICKLY POINT PIT STOP

QUICKSAND GULCH

RACING RIVER

START

FINISH

OIL SLICK ALLEY

Scale: 1 in = 20 mi

1. Use the data on the table to find:

   a. mean_____

   b. median_____

   c. range _____

   d. mode _____

HOW MUCH PIZZA DO YOU EAT PER MONTH?

LAUREN	4
RAUL	8
YOKO	4
SAL	7
PAM	9
TYE	4

2. Solve the problem.

$$7.63 \times 2.48 =$$

3. Rico's pizza chef can prepare a pizza for baking in four minutes. At that rate, how many pizzas can the chef make in an hour? _____ in three hours? _____

4. Match the figure to the correct label.

___ rectangular prism ___ pyramid ___ cube ___ cylinder

a.   b.   c.   d.

5. Find the area of Rico's sign without the frame.

 = 6 sq. in

Rico's Pizzaria

Best Pizza in Town

OPEN 7 DAYS A WEEK
11 AM – 11 PM

1. Write this numeral:

fifty-three million, one hundred sixteen thousand, forty-three

2. Three fifths of Monday night's pizza was left over. Emmy ate $\frac{1}{3}$ of it for lunch on Tuesday. How much pizza still remained? ____

3. Verify the solution. Correct it if necessary.

$$7r + 6 = 62$$
$$r = 8$$

4. Use a protractor to measure the angle of each slice of pizza.

a. _____ °   b. _____ °   c. _____ °

5. Jess and Hannah bought groceries to prepare pizza and brought home a torn receipt. How much did the mozzarella cheese cost? _____

```
Shop Right Market
     4-1-07
_____
Tomato sauce........$0.99
Tomato paste........$0.78
Mozzarella cheese...$3.
Parmesan cheese.....$1.85

Total:............ $7.45
```

1. Which statement is an example of the zero property of multiplication?

a. 16 x 0 = 0   c. 47 x 0 = 47
b. 0 x 139 = 139 x 0   d. 0 + 72 = 72

2. Match the figure to the correct label.

_____ ray   _____ line segment   _____ line

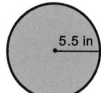

3. Evan spent $\frac{2}{3}$ of his $5.25 lunch money on two slices of pizza, and the rest on a large orange juice. What is the cost:

a. of a pizza slice _____ ?
b. of the juice _____ ?

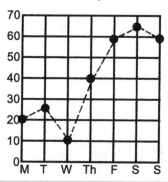

5.5 in

4. The diameter of this pizza = ____ in

The circumference of the pizza = ____ in

5. Which statement is true about pizza sales for the week?

a. More pizzas were sold on Sunday than on any other day.
b. Monday was the lowest day of sales.
c. Wednesday's low sales must mean that pizza recipes need to improve.
d. More pizzas are sold on weekends than on weekdays.

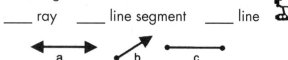

1. Estimate the shaded part of each figure using $\frac{4}{5}$, $\frac{2}{3}$, $\frac{1}{2}$, or $\frac{1}{3}$.

a___   b___   c___   d___

2. Solve the problem.   **4.32 ÷ 1.2 =**

3. Simplify and solve.   **5m + 2m – m = 54**

4. The package of mozzarella cheese weighs ___ pounds, ___ ounces.
(Hint: 1 pound = 16 oz)

Cheese
53 oz.

5. a. The total number of students surveyed was 253. How many students prefer Meat Lovers Pizza? _____

c. Complete the bar graph.

7TH GRADE PIZZA PREFERENCES

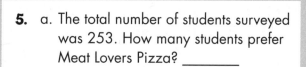

1. What will the sixth figure look like? Draw it.

2. The pizzas came out of the oven at 5:25 p.m. They had baked for 18 minutes. At what time were they placed in the oven? _____

3. Solve the problem.   **657 x 83 =**

4. Johnny Ariani's giant pizza usually serves five adults. At that rate, how many should he prepare for a group of 64 adults? _____

5. Challenge Problem

The largest pizza ever made was baked at the Norwood Hypermarket in Johannesburg, South Africa, and was 122 feet, 8 inches in diameter.

    a. Use a calculator to help you compare the ingredients used in an average 15-inch pizza with those used in the world's largest pizza. Complete the table.

       (Hints: 1 C = 16 T, 1 lb = 16 oz; 1 gal = 16 C)

Ingredient	Amount in 15-in. pizza	Amount in World's Largest Pizza
Flour	3 C	_____C (cups)
Tomato Sauce	3 C	____C = ____gal, ____qt, ____C
Mozzarella cheese	8 oz	____ oz = ____lbs, ____ oz
Pepperoni	4 oz	____ oz = ____ lbs, ____ oz
Serves	four	_____(make an educated guess)

    b. Use a formula to find the circumference of each pizza: **15-inch diameter, C = _____ in**

                                                  122 foot, 8 inch diameter, C = _____ in

    c. Use a string and yardstick to measure the shoulder span of a classmate. _____ inches

    d. About how many students of similar size could stand shoulder to shoulder around the edge of the world's largest pizza? _____

1. Jean Pierre Blanchard, the first person to ascend in a hot air balloon in America, stayed in the air for forty-five minutes while George Washington watched. Shade 45 minutes on the clock. What fraction of the clock is shaded?

a. $\frac{2}{3}$ b. $\frac{5}{8}$ c. $\frac{3}{4}$ d. not here

2. Bert Piccard and Brian Jones piloted a hot air balloon across the Pacific Ocean. The balloon moved at a rate of 115 miles per hour and traveled for six days. How many miles did the men travel in their balloon?

3. Solve the problem. $20 \overline{)3085}$

4. At the water balloon toss, one out of every five balloons broke before the game began. Out of 65 balloons, how many broke before the game?
(Hint: You can set up your problem as an equivalent fraction: $\frac{1}{5} = $)

5. Match each figure with its description.

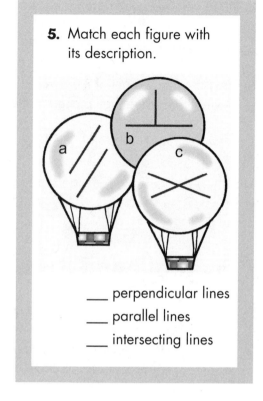

___ perpendicular lines
___ parallel lines
___ intersecting lines

1. Last week forty-nine percent of the 228 helium balloons sold at Peg's Party Store had the words "Happy Birthday."

a. Estimate the number of birthday balloons sold. _____
b. Compute the actual number sold. _____
c. How close was your estimate? _____

2. Solve the problem. $2\frac{3}{8} + 3\frac{1}{4} =$

3. Per Lindstrand reached this altitude in feet when he set the world record for height in his hot air balloon: 60,000 + 4,000 + 900 + 90 + 7. Write the number in standard form.

4. Use the number line and complete the function table for the given rule.

-10 -9 -8 -7 -6 -5 -4 -3 -2 -1 0 1 2 3 4 5 6 7 8 9 10

Input	Output
2	
0	
-1	
-3	

Output = Input + 7

5. Use a ruler to draw the following line segments.

a. CD = $2\frac{3}{4}$ in
b. FG = $1\frac{5}{8}$ in
c. PQ = 3.2 cm

WEDNESDAY WEEK 18 _____ MATH PRACTICE
Name

1. The hot air balloon touched down at 9:51 a.m. It had been in the air for 1 hour and 35 minutes. What time did the balloon ascend?

2. Round each numeral to the hundreds place and estimate the sum.

$$\begin{array}{r} 1,687 \\ 428 \\ + 2,981 \\ \hline \end{array}$$

3. Weather balloons released from 950 stations around the world keep records of the earth's atmosphere. Write this number in the blank in exponential form.

(9 x _____) + 50 = 950

4. The balloons are _____
   a. similar   c. matched
   b. cylinders   d. congruent

5. Allissa and Alex distributed free helium balloons to preschoolers at their school's winter fair. Use the graph to tell how many more blue balloons than pink were given away. _____

Balloons Given Away

Red	
Blue	
Pink	
Orange	
Green	
Key:	= 3 balloons

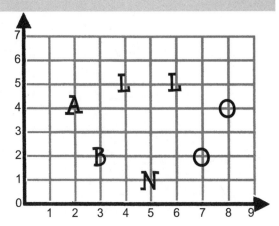

THURSDAY WEEK 18 _____ MATH PRACTICE
Name

1. Solve the problem.   **146.2 – 94.35 =**

2. A weather balloon at a height of 6,000 feet recorded a temperature of 23°F. Another balloon at 10,000 feet recorded a temperature of –5°F. What was the difference between the two recorded temperatures? _____

3. Round each decimal to the nearest tenth.
   a. 63.13_____
   b. .094 _____
   c. 12.47_____

4. Cindy Johnson's hot air balloon can lift up to 220 kilograms. Cindy weighs 59 kg and her copilot weighs 62 kg. How many kilograms of cargo can the women carry in their balloon?

5. Write the coordinates for each letter in the word "Balloon."

   B _____   A _____
   L _____   L _____
   O _____   O _____
   N _____

Solve the problems for 1–4. Use the alphabet code to find the name of the hot air balloon. Find the letter that matches the answer to each problem. Write the letters (in order) on the balloon.

1. $(3 \times 6^2) + 9 =$ _____

2. a. $7,488 \div 24 =$ _____

   b. $1.888 \div 0.8 =$ _____

3. a. Write as a percent: $\frac{1}{4} =$ ____%

   b. Find that percent of 60 ____

4. a. $5.9 \times 0.4 =$ _____

   b. $0.9 \times 0.6 =$ _____

A	B	C	D	E	F	G	H	I	J	K	L	M	N	O	P	Q	R	S	T	U	V	W	X	Y	Z
39	55	45	14	148	0.02	14.75	25	15	38	312	3.1	12	0.9	26	4464	187	0.6	117	0.236	318	47	1.25	236	2.35	1.8

5. Challenge Problem

The guests at Marla's 21st birthday celebration released 21 helium balloons in her honor. The pink balloons, one-third of the total, were released first. One-seventh of the remaining balloons were pale blue. After these were released, one-third of those left were yellow. When the yellow balloons were released, one-fourth of the balloons left were lavender. The rest were lime green. How many balloons of each color were there?

   a. Use the pattern to cut 21 balloons out of scrap paper.
   b. Use your cutout balloons to solve the problem.
   c. Color the balloons with the correct colors.

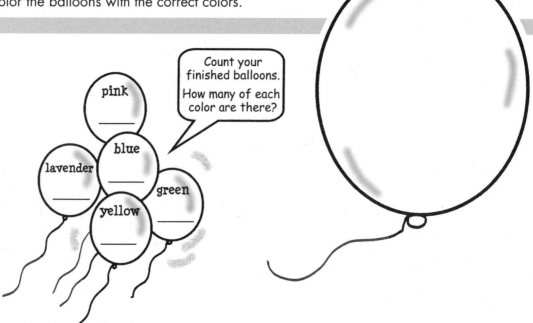

MONDAY WEEK 19 _____ MATH PRACTICE

1. Each summer, about 20,000 people visit Mount Rushmore each day to admire the huge heads of presidents. Use mental math to estimate the number of visitors to the site during the first twenty days of July.

2. Find the label to match each figure. Write the letter on the figure.

   (p) pentagon
   (h) hexagon
   (r) rhombus
   (o) octagon

3. Solve. Show the remainder:

   595 ÷ 31 =

4. Find the surface area of the cube if the area of one of its faces is 81 square inches.

5. On his hike around Mt. St. Helens, Jacob carried water and orange juice in his backpack. He also carried peanut butter bars, crackers, and energy bars. When he stopped for his first break, he ate one snack and drank one kind of liquid. Make a list of all the possible combinations he might have consumed.

Mmm, goodies.

TUESDAY WEEK 19 _____ MATH PRACTICE

1. The climbers reached the summit of Mt. Marcy at 11:07 a.m. after climbing for three hours and twenty minutes. At what time did they begin their climb?

It's a-boot time.

2. Solve the equation.

   y − 16 = 29
   y =

	X1	X2	X3	X4	X5	X6	X7	X8	X9	X10	X11	X12
6												
8												

3. Which operation would you use to compare the size of two mountains?

   a. addition   c. multiplication
   b. subtraction   d. division

4. Use mental math to solve the problems.
   a. 19,000 ÷ 100 =
   b. 19,000 ÷ 10 =

5. Use the multiples chart for these tasks:
   a. Finish the chart by writing the multiples of 6 and 8.
   b. Circle the common multiples of 6 and 8.
   c. Draw a square around the LCM (Least Common Multiple).

Name

1. Draw a pentagon.

2. Mt. Everest, in Nepal, is 29,035 feet high. How many yards high is Mt. Everest?

3. Which kind of graph would best compare the sizes of the tallest mountain peaks in the western United States?

      a. bar   b. circle   c. line   d. picture

4. Abe Lincoln's mouth carved into Mt. Rushmore is 18 feet wide. Is the grid's scale reasonable?____ Explain why or why not.

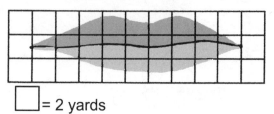

☐ = 2 yards

5. Sharon put aside $100.00 to purchase some mountaineering supplies online from a mountaineering supply site. She bought an axe and one pair of mittens. How much remained after paying her bill?

_____

MOUNTAINEERING CATALOG 2007

Sale!

$55.00 ICE AXE

POLAR FLEECE MITTENS
$22.00

SHIPPING & HANDLING – $10.50

What a sweet deal!

Name

1. A sudden storm on Mt. McKinley caused the temperature to drop from 75°F to 28°F in a matter of minutes. Which equations would help find the temperature change?

    a. $75 - x = 28$ b. $28 + 75 = x$

            c. $75 - 28 = x$

2. Match the fraction with the decimal that has the same value.

    a. $\frac{3}{6}$ = _____   0.8

    b. $\frac{1}{8}$ = _____   0.25

    c. $\frac{4}{5}$ = _____   0.5

    d. $\frac{1}{4}$ = _____   0.125

3. Use the number line to solve: **3 – 9 =**

-7 -6 -5 -4 -3 -2 -1 0 1 2 3 4 5 6 7

4. Hawaii's Mt. Kea is 31,000 feet high, but only 13,680 feet of the mountain are above sea level. How many feet of Mt. Kea are under the ocean?

5. What words should be written in the empty space on the Venn diagram below?

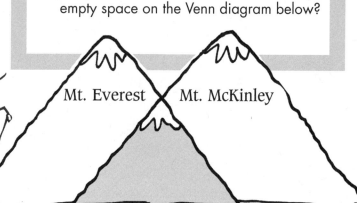

Mt. Everest   Mt. McKinley

1. Solve the problem.

$$\begin{array}{r} 146 \\ \times\ 38 \\ \hline \end{array}$$

2. Choose the appropriate equation and solve the problem.

The group leader divided 7 granola bars in half so all the climbers could have a small snack during a rest top. How many climbers were served?

a. $\frac{1}{2} \times 7 =$

b. $\frac{1}{2} \div 7 =$

c. $7 \div \frac{1}{2} =$

3. Which is not a prime number?

17   13   7   11   5   2   9

4. There are 109 mountain peaks in the world are over 24,000 feet high. Ninety-six of these are in the Himalayan mountain range. What percentage of the world's largest peaks would be found in the Himalayas?

I'm only 23,999 feet tall.

5. Challenge Problem

The Highest Mountain on Each Continent

CONTINENT	NAME OF MOUNTAIN	HEIGHT IN METERS
AFRICA	MT. KILIMANJARO	5,895
ANTARCTICA	VINSON MASSIF	4,897
ASIA	MT. EVEREST	8,850
AUSTRALIA	MT. KOSCUISKO	2,228
EUROPE	MT. ELBRUS	5,642
N. AMERICA	MT. McKINLEY	6,194
S. AMERICA	MT. ANACAGUA	6,960

a. Study the table.

b. Complete the bar graph to show the approximate height of each continent's tallest peak in meters.

c. Write three questions that would require a student to use the information on your graph.

d. Turn your paper upside down and write the answers to your three questions.

COMPARISON OF HIGHEST PEAKS IN EACH CONTINENT

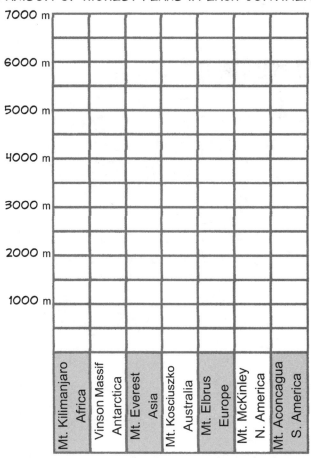

1. Which shows the distributive property?

    a. (6 x 4) + 3 = 6 x (4 + 3)

    b. (6 x 4) + 3 = 27

    c. 6 x (4 + 3) = (6 x 4) + (6 x 3)

2. This heart has _____ line(s) of symmetry.

3. On Monday, Maria exercised for 25 minutes. Tuesday's time was 5 minutes more than Monday's. Wednesday's time was five 5 more than Tuesday's. She continued the pattern for the next 4 days. How many minutes did she exercise on Sunday?

4. Draw hands on the second clock to show what the time will be in 2 hours and 10 minutes.

5. Dylan tosses this cube each day to choose an after-school activity. What are his chances of landing on an aerobic activity? Write your answer as a lowest terms fraction. (Two views of the same cube are pictured.)

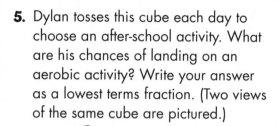

Aerobic is anything that exercises your heart.

1. Solve the problem.

$$3\frac{1}{4}$$
$$+2\frac{2}{3}$$

I didn't calculate on that.

2. If all of your blood vessels were joined end to end, they'd stretch for sixty thousand miles! Which of the following is another way of writing this number of miles?

    a. 6×10^2 c. 6×10^5

    b. 6×10^4 d. 6×10^3

3. In 1628 William Harvey, an English physician discovered that the heart is a pump that moves blood through the body. How many years ago did Dr. Harvey make his discovery? _____

4. Solve the equation if n = 9

    4 + 2 n = _____

5. Read the information about the surgeries performed by three heart surgeons during the second week in May. Tell the number performed by each doctor.

Dr. Chow performed two more operations than Dr. Reinhardt. Dr. Forbes was on vacation part of the week and performed only $\frac{1}{3}$ as many operations as Dr. Reinhardt. In all, the doctors did 58 heart operations.

    a. Dr. C = _____

    b. Dr. R = _____

    c. Dr. F = _____

Listen to your heart.

S	M	T	W	TH	F	S
					1	2
3	4	5	6	7	8	9
10	11	12	13	14	15	16
17	18	19	20	21	22	23
24	25	26	27	28	29	30

1. The average heart beats about 70 times per minute. At that rate, how many times does it beat in one hour? _____ in one day? _____

2. Solve the problem.

26.3 + 19 + 148.25 =

3. Which of these describe the figure?
   a. isosceles triangle
   b. equilateral triangle
   c. scalene triangle

4. Normal body temperature is 98.6°F. When Sulee had the flu, her temperature rose to 102.4° F. Find the difference between this and her normal body temperature.

RESTING HEART RATES

Name	Rate (bpm)
Heather	69
Heidi	72
Ryan	71
Chelsea	72

5. a. The range of bpm for the four kids is _____

   b. The mean number of bpm is _____

You make my heart beat faster.

1. Write the numeral for **five hundred seventy four and fifty two hundredths**.

2. Round each numeral to the thousands place and estimate the sum.

21,589 + 18,112 + 37,941 =

3. Each year 719,000 people in the U. S. die of heart disease. Seventy percent of these people have coronary heart disease. How many people die of coronary heart disease each year in the United States? _____

4. Simplify and solve:

6 + (5 + 9) − (4 + 2) =

5. When resting, the average heart pumps three quarts of blood each minute. At that rate, how many gallons of blood does the heart pump in . . .

an hour? _____

a day? _____

a week? _____

Wow, that's impressive pumping.

1. Solve the problem.

$$(5 + 9) \times 4 + 3 =$$

2. Write each in lowest terms.

a. $\frac{12}{16}$ = _____

b. $\frac{9}{30}$ = _____

c. $\frac{12}{2}$ = _____

3. a. Write the factors for 20 and 30.

b. What is the GCF (greatest common factor)?

4. Measure the height of the heart. Then use the scale to determine the real height of the average adult human heart.

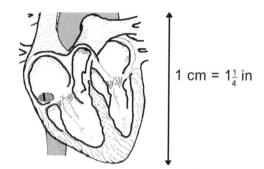

$1 \text{ cm} = 1\frac{1}{4} \text{ in}$

5. Challenge Problem

Brian Ferguson, a college basketball captain, wore a monitor that recorded his heart rate for an entire day. Create a table that organizes the information Brian gathered about his heart.

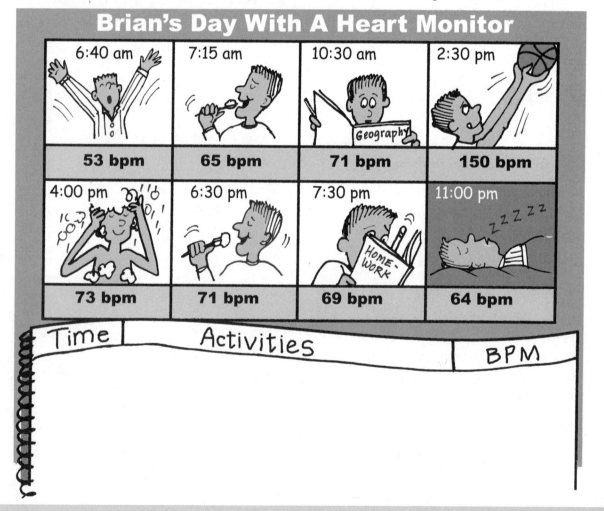

Brian's Day With A Heart Monitor

6:40 am	7:15 am	10:30 am	2:30 pm
53 bpm	65 bpm	71 bpm	150 bpm
4:00 pm	6:30 pm	7:30 pm	11:00 pm
73 bpm	71 bpm	69 bpm	64 bpm

Time	Activities	BPM

MONDAY WEEK 21 _____ MATH PRACTICE

Name

1. Solve the problem.

$100 – $59.35 =

$MILE

2. Write **>**, **<**, or **=** in each circle.

a. 35 in ⬤ 1yd   c. 5 qt ⬤ 1 gal

b. 4 hrs ⬤ 220 min   d. 96 cm ⬤ 1m

3. The Gobi Desert is 1600 km wide from east to west and 100 km long from north to south. Use the formula (**A = l x w**) to find the area of the desert.

4. Measure the angles of the sand dunes.

Angle A = _____°   Angle B = _____°

Angle C = _____°

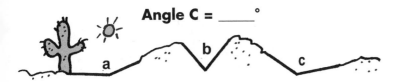

5. Use the table to find the following:

a. range _____

b. median _____

c. mode _____

d. mean _____

Daily Low Temperatures
Gobi Desert
First Week of January

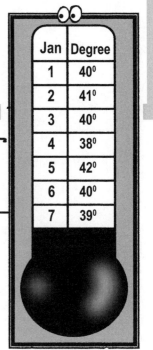

Jan	Degree
1	40°
2	41°
3	40°
4	38°
5	42°
6	40°
7	39°

TUESDAY WEEK 21 _____ MATH PRACTICE

Name

1. Solve the problem.

$$4\frac{1}{4} \times 3 =$$

2. Which is **not** divisible by 3?

a. 120   b. 32   c. 60   d. 123

3. Deserts get less than **254 mm** of annual rainfall. This measurement is . . .

a. 2.54 cm   c. 0.254 cm

b. 2540 cm   d. 25.4 cm

4. Find the value of **s** if **r** = 9

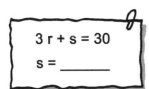

3 r + s = 30

s = _____

5. The Sahara desert's sand dunes can be as high as 200 meters. Sketch a 200-meter dune to scale on the grid.

That dune is how tall?

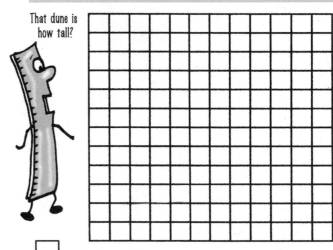

⬜ = 20 meters

1. Choose the best unit to measure the mass (weight) of each of the following. Write milligram (mg) gram (g) or kilogram (kg).

a. two math books _____   c. a child _____

b. 3 paper clips _____   d. a tissue _____

2. What is the measure of angle C? (*Hint: The angles of a triangle total 180°.*)

3. Solve the problem.

15.4 x 12.8 =

4. Marcus kept track of the time he spent catching lizards in the desert over four days. How long did he do this? ____hrs ____min

Mon.	Tues.	Wed.	Thurs.
55 min	42 min	24 min	1 hr, 10 min

Amount of Water Five Students Drank on a Mojave Desert Hike   = 8 oz

8-9 am	
9-10 am	
10-11 am	
11 am-noon	

5. a. How many more ounces of water were drunk between 11 a.m. and noon than between 8 and 9 a.m.? ____

b. They drank twice as much water between ____ and _____ as they did between _____ and _____ .

1. Use the number line to solve this problem. **−8 + 4 =**

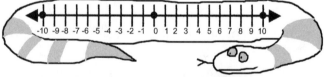

2. The area of the shaded triangle is _____

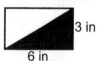

3 in
6 in

3. Order the numerals from least to greatest.

20.2   0.02   2.2   0.2   0.022   22.2

4. Study the pattern on the cacti. Continue the pattern on the fourth cactus.

5. The Atacama Desert in Chile is the driest place in the world and gets precipitation only two to four times each century! Which of the following statements about the Atacama Desert is probably **not** true?

a. It's unlikely it will rain more than 8 times in the Atacama during my lifetime.

b. The Atacama Desert has no lakes.

c. It has rained about 20 times in the Atacama since the Pilgrims landed at Plymouth Rock in 1620.

d. It's not possible to calculate the average amount of yearly precipitation in the Atacama.

1. Use mental math to solve the problem to find the area of Argentina's Patagonia Desert.

$$15 \times 2 \times 10^4 = \_\_\_\_\ mi^2$$

2. Of the 20,000 square miles in the Mojave Desert, 2,388 are located in the Mojave National Preserve. How many square miles of the Mojave are **not** in the national preserve?

_____

3. The world's largest desert, the Sahara, is **nine million one hundred thousand** square kilometers, an area as large as the whole continental United States! Write this numeral as a standard numeral.

4. Will purchased these four books on desert snakes for a total. How much change did he receive from a $50 bill?

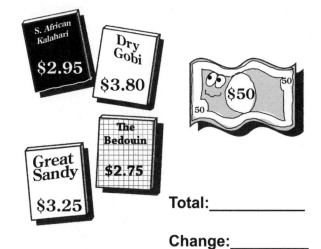

Total:_____

Change:_____

5. Challenge Problem

1. Draw four pictures (of the desert items shown) at locations of your choice on the "desert" grid. Make sure you draw each one at a place where two lines on the grid intersect. Label these pictures B, C, D, and E.

2. Then draw a path through the desert. Begin at Point A and end at Point F. Your path must connect each of the drawings.

3. Write the coordinates for each point on your path.

A_____
B_____
C_____
D_____
E_____
F_____

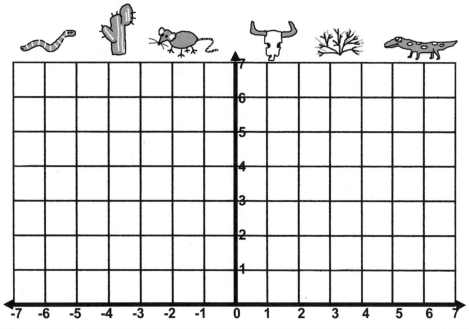

1. In April 1974 a record number of tornadoes (148) swept through the southern and midwestern United States over a 24-hour period. What was the average number of tornadoes per hour on that unusual day?

2. How many faces are on each figure?

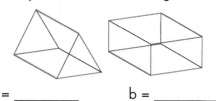

a = _____   b = _____

3. Solve the problem:

4417 ÷ 35

4. Each side of an octagon measures 1.2 centimeters. Estimate the perimeter.

1.2 cm

Tornado crossing!

5. The 800 students at St. Thomas High School voted to choose a name for their basketball team.

a. How many students voted for the name *Hurricanes*? _____

b. How many more chose *Tornadoes* than chose *Cyclones*? _____

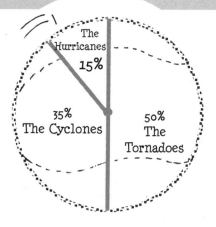

The Hurricanes 15%

35% The Cyclones

50% The Tornadoes

1. Each year about 1143 tornadoes form around the world. Seventy percent of them occur in the United States. About how many tornadoes take place in the U. S. each year?

2. Solve the problem.

$3.2\overline{)13.6}$

3. A waterspout is like a tornado, but it occurs over water. Find the perimeter of a waterspout that is 5 meters in diameter.

4. Order the fractions from greatest to least.

$\frac{2}{5}$ $\frac{1}{2}$ $\frac{3}{4}$ $\frac{7}{10}$

5. Which statement matches the expression?

(15 + p) x 3

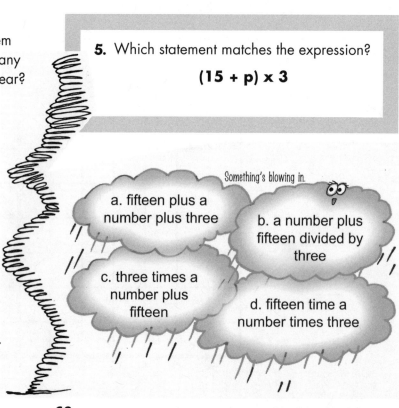

Something's blowing in.

a. fifteen plus a number plus three

b. a number plus fifteen divided by three

c. three times a number plus fifteen

d. fifteen time a number times three

1. Which two shapes are congruent?

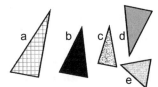

2. **39.2 – 16.24 = 22.96**
The solution above is ___correct ___incorrect.

3. On a rare occasion, a tornado can be as great as **2 km** in diameter. This is _____ **m**.

4. A bag has 5 brown, 8 red, 3 yellow, and 4 green M & M's. If you randomly select one, what are your chances of getting red or green?

5. Maya used cubes to create a word that comes to mind when she thinks of tornadoes. Which letter(s) has a volume . . .
a. of 11 cubic units? _____
b. of 8 cubic units? _____

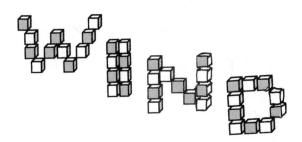

1. During a period of extensive storms in the Midwestern U. S., a team of storm chasers might work up to 1.5 days without stopping to rest. How many hours might the storm chasers work?

_____

2. Add a ( ) and two operational signs {+, – , x , or ÷ } to make the expression true.

3 2 8 = 40

3. Which two fractions are equivalent?

$\frac{2}{3}$ $\frac{1}{5}$ $\frac{1}{2}$ $\frac{4}{1}$ $\frac{3}{15}$

4. Solve the problem. Verify your answer on the number line.

4 – 9 = _____

5. The Kansas map shows two cities that experienced tornadoes on the same day one summer. Use the scale of miles to estimate how far apart the tornadoes were. _____

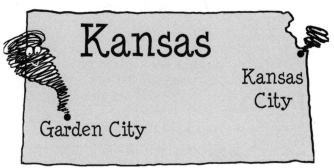

1 in = 130 m

1. What is the lowest common multiple (LCM) for 3 and 5?

Catch me if you can!

2. Which operation can be added to the circle to make the equation true?

(5 x 8) ◯ (17 + 3) = 6 x 10

3. Joshua Wurman chased storms for recreation for three years before he decided to earn his living at it. In all, he's chased storms for twelve years. Write a fraction (in lowest terms) that compares his recreational storm chasing to the total number of years he's chased storms.

4. Write the fraction from problem #3 . . .

a. . . . as a decimal _____

b. . . . as a percent _____

5. Challenge Problem

Four families live in a row on Sweet Street. A wild tornado swept through this quiet neighborhood last week. It was fortunate that no lives were lost, though the fierce winds caused the strange relocation of some objects. One of these happened for each of the families:

- **One family's pet boa constrictor ended up wrapped around the downtown courthouse clock tower.**
- **Another family's bathtub was found in a tree on Main Street.**
- **A cow from a farm in the next county was deposited (through the smashed roof) into one garage.**
- **Another neighbor found a stop sign from a nearby town planted in its front yard.**

Follow the clues below to figure out which family lives in which house, the color of the house, and the strange relocation affecting that family.

Clues:

- The Smiths live next door to the Ruiz family.
- The missing boa was from the red house.
- The stop sign landed in the yard of the family that lives next door to where the cow landed in the garage.
- The Bernsteins live in a green house.

- The missing bathtub came from a brown house.
- The white house is between the red and green houses.
- The Ruiz family does not have a garage.
- The digits in the Bernstein's house number have a sum of 5.
- The Smiths lost their boa constrictor.
- The McCalls do not live in a white house.

1. Use a protractor to measure the angle formed by the V of the migrating birds.

2. With its long legs and neck, an ostrich can be 270 cm tall. This measurement is equal to

a. 2.7 m   b. 27 m   c. 0.27 m

3. Use the order of operations to solve. *(Hint: Use this order: parenthesis, exponents, multiplication, division, addition, subtraction.)*

$$17 - (5 + 6) + (4 \times 9) =$$

4. Subtract to solve. Add in reverse to verify.

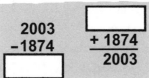

```
 2003        [    ]
-1874       + 1874
[    ]        2003
```

5. Erika wanted to draw a bird. She decided the bird would be sitting on either a fence or a tree. She thought about drawing either a robin, a jay, or a cardinal. She decided she'd have the bird eating a beetle or a worm. Finish the tree diagram to find the number of possibilities for her drawing.

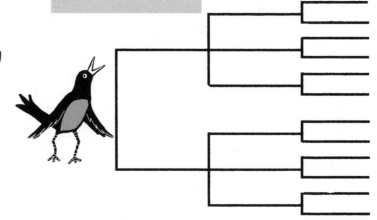

1. The smallest flying bird, the hummingbird, weighs only **1.6 grams** while the largest flying bird, the bustard, weighs **18 kilograms**. How much more does a bustard weigh than a hummingbird?

2. Solve the problem.

$$23\frac{1}{5}$$
$$- 14\frac{3}{5}$$

3. An emperor penguin can dive 250 meters and stay under the water for 12 minutes. Write a fraction to show the part of an hour a penguin can stay submerged.

4. Find and continue the pattern.

1, 3, 7, 21, 25, 75, 79, ____ , ____

5. A pheasant lays 15 eggs during each nesting season. Let s stand for a number of seasons. Which expression could you use to find how many eggs a pheasant would lay during any number of seasons?

a. 15 + s

b. 15 − s

c. 15 ÷ s

d. 15 x s

1. Use mental math to solve.

A peregrine falcon can fly at a speed of 200 miles per hour. At that rate, how long will it take the falcon to fly 1,400 miles? _____

2. Name the figures.

 a   b   c

3. Solve the problem.

$$571 \times 382 =$$

4. Students from Pinehurst School took a field trip to the Klamath Bird Refuge. They arrived at the refuge at 9:10 a.m. and followed the activities shown on the chart at the right. What time did they arrive back at school?_____

5. Elena, Kacie, Grace, and Christine went on the bird refuge field trip and sat together as pairs on the bus. List all the possible seating combinations for the four girls.

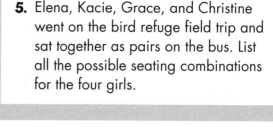

Activity	Time Spent
Visitors' Center	45 min
Bird watching at marsh	1 hr, 55 min
Picnic lunch	35 min
Sketching shore birds	50 min
Endangered species lecture	40 min
Drive back to school	1 hr, 15 min

1. Circle the composite numbers.

12   15   6   11
5   21   3   2

2. The aviary director at the Lincoln Zoo is ordering new fencing to place around the pentagon-shaped ostrich pen. Each side of the pen measures 19 ft. How many yards of fencing will he need to order? _____

3. The fencing (#2 above) is sold in 5-yd sections. Each section costs $64.00. How much will it cost to fence the ostrich pen?

4. Use trial and error to find the value of **b**.

$$4b + 6 = 34$$

5. What is the total amount of money shown? _____

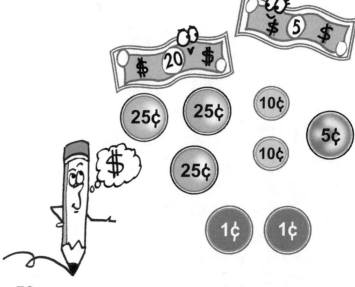

1. Use the associative property to find the value of n.

$$14 \times (6 \times 12) = (14 \times n) \times 12$$
$$n = \underline{\quad}$$

2. An emperor penguin lays her egg in the coldest part of winter when the temperature is – 80 degrees F. How many degrees below freezing is that? _____

3. Write **7,205** in word form.

_____

_____

4. The number of birds Ashley spotted each of four days is:

   AND 95

FIND THE MEAN: _____

5. Challenge Problem

An American woodcock, a crow, a falcon, and an eagle, all from Los Angeles, CA are planning to meet at the Winged Friends Convention in San Francisco's Golden Gate Park on June 5th. The distance from Los Angeles to San Francisco if 350 miles. The convention begins at 9:00 a.m. on Monday, but the birds want to arrive at 8:30 a.m. for a little preening and snack before the opening speech.

a. Notice the speed at which each bird is capable of flying. Then calculate the amount of travel time for each of the birds and tell when they should leave home in order to make it by 8:30 a.m. on June 5th. Complete the table with your calculations.

b. Write a ratio to compare
(1) the speed of the falcon to the speed of the eagle _____
(2) the speed of the woodcock to the crow's speed _____

c. Admission to the conference is $65.00 per bird, but there's a 10% discount for those who pay before June 1st. The eagle has offered to pay for all her friends and will be sure to pay before the first of June. Find the admission cost for all four of them. _____

Distance from Los Angeles to San Francisco: 350 miles

Bird	Flying Speed	Travel Time from L.A. to San Francisco	When To Leave Home
American Woodcock	5 mph		
crow	25 mph		
eagle	50 mph		
falcon	200 mph		

Name

1. The dotted line shows that the skateboard deck is

    a. congruent   c. symmetrical

    b. rectangular   d. similar

2. Solve the problem.

$$\frac{2}{3} \times 3\frac{1}{8} =$$

3. Which is the best estimate for the number of milliliters (ml) a skateboarder would drink after a competition in the hot summer sun?

    a. 1,500   b. 150   c. 15,000   d. 15

4. Tony Hawk, world champion skateboarder, won 3 silver, 3 bronze, and 9 gold medals at the 2003 X Games.

    a. Write a fraction (in lowest terms) comparing gold medals to the total number. _____

    b. Write the above fraction as a percent _____

5. Take one spin. What is the probability of spinning . . .

    a. an even number?_____

    b. a number less than 6?_____

    c. a prime number?_____

My head's spinning.

Name

1. Of the top 10 female skateboarders in the 2004 World Cup, 9 came from the U. S. They earned a total of 14,750 points. Write this number in words.

2. Solve the problem.

$$\frac{3}{5} \div \frac{1}{3} =$$

3. Eighteen students each have a skateboard. $\frac{1}{6}$ are black, $\frac{1}{3}$ are white, and the rest of the boards are red. How many boards are . . .

    a. black? _____

    b. white? _____

    c. red? _____

4. Simplify the expression. Then find the value of n.

$$5n - 2n = 15$$

$$n = \underline{\qquad}$$

5. Brent ordered a helmet, knee pads, and wrist guards on the Internet. Use a formula to find the volume of the delivery box.

I'll skate right over.

8 in

10 in

Skatemate Accessories

To: B.Brown
123 Elm Street
Tiny Town, U.S.A.

12 in

1. Rob wants to buy the following Tony Hawk mementos: photo ($4.50), key chain ($3.95), Video ($12.95), water bottle ($2.75), DVD ($14.95). Can he get these all for $30?

2. What is the circumference of a skateboard wheel with a diameter of 2.5 inches?

3. Round each numeral to its greatest place value and estimate the answer.

$$2,116 + 896 + 3,724 =$$

4. Draw a line from each figure to its name.

a. line
b. point
c. plane
d. ray
e. line segment

I really flipped!

5. Nate made a graph to record his best skateboarding speed for each of the spring and summer months.

a. What was his speed range between April and September? _____

b. Between what months did Nate make the greatest improvement?

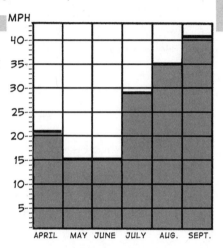

1. Solve the problem.

$$12.9 + 32.73 + 0.05 =$$

2. The Kent City Council voted to build a new skateboard park. Its dimensions will be 120 ft by 85 ft. Find . . .

    a. the park's area_____

    b. the park's perimeter_____

3. Kendra has been skateboarding for *m* years. Her younger brother, Nick, has been skateboarding for two years less. How many years has Nick skateboarded? Which expression matches the situation?

    a. 2 m   b. m – 2   c. m + 2   d. m ÷ 2

4. Solve problem #5 and fill in these blanks.

Nora got _____ out of _____ correct on her weight quiz. She has _____ percent correct.

Measure up.

5. Check Nora's quiz. Write the correct answer in place of each incorrect one.

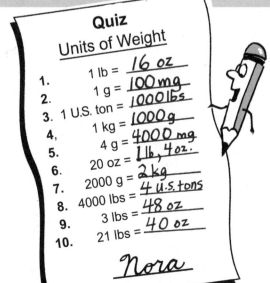

Quiz
Units of Weight

1. 1 lb = 16 oz
2. 1 g = 100 mg
3. 1 U.S. ton = 1000 lbs
4. 1 kg = 1000 g
5. 4 g = 4000 mg
6. 20 oz = 1 lb, 4 oz.
7. 2000 g = 2 kg
8. 4000 lbs = 4 U.S. tons
9. 3 lbs = 48 oz
10. 21 lbs = 40 oz

Nora

Top Ten Male Vert Skaters 2004

Name	Country	Points
Sandro Dias	Brazil	6000
Neal Hendrix	U. S.	4375
Andy MacDonald	U.S.	4350
Lincoln Ueda	Brazil	4275
Rune Glifberg	Denmark	4150
Rodrigo Menezes	Brazil	4025
Mike Crum	U.S.	3925
Bob Burnquist	Brazil	2900
Jake Brown	Australia	2875
Juergen Horrwarth	Germany	2725

Accumulated High Scores Per Country

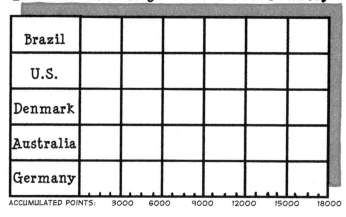

Brazil						
U.S.						
Denmark						
Australia						
Germany						

ACCUMULATED POINTS: 3000 6000 9000 12000 15000 18000

1. Find the total number of points earned by each of the countries that made it into the top ten.

Brazil_____   United States_____   Denmark_____   Australia_____   Germany_____

2. Find the difference between the total number of points earned by Brazil and the United States. _____

3. Write Brazil's total points as an expanded numeral.

4. Fill in the bar graph to show the points for each country.

5. Challenge Problem

a. Use a blue crayon or marker to trace any hexagons in the pattern on the skateboard.

b. Use red to trace any parallelograms.

c. Use green to trace any triangles.

d. Use yellow to trace trapezoids.

e. Use orange to trace a symmetrical figure and draw one line of symmetry.

f. Color the design with at least three different colors.

1. The General Sherman giant Sequoia in California's redwood forest has a radius of 13 feet. Find . . .

    a. its diameter

    b. its circumference

2. Add <, >, or = to make the equation true.

(29 – 4) x 3 ◯ (15 x 6) – 10

3. In April of 2003, a group of 96 British school children and adults planted 4,100 trees in one hour. If they kept a steady pace, how many trees were planted each minute?

4. What is the probability of spinning an oak with one spin?

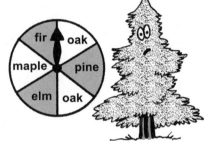

5. Find the coordinates for the following:

    tree frog   _____

    pine cone   _____

    maple leaf   _____

    squirrel   _____

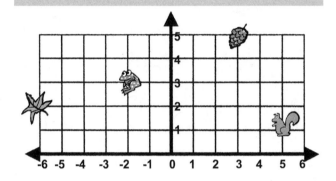

1. List all of the factors of 40.

2. Which sign makes the expression true?

(125 ◯ 25) + 30 = 35

    a. x   b. +   c. ÷   d. –

3. A poplar tree grows 3 mm every day. At that rate, how many **centimeters** will a poplar grow in the month of April?

4. Find the area of the top surface of a tree stump with a 16-inch diameter.

16 in

5. The answer is 12. Which of these could be the problem?

Chopping is hard work!

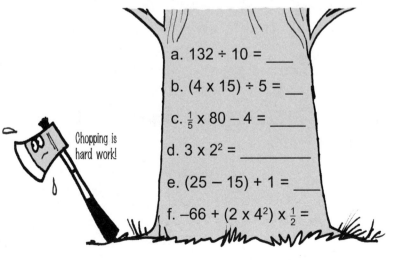

a. $132 \div 10 =$ ___

b. $(4 \times 15) \div 5 =$ ___

c. $\frac{1}{5} \times 80 - 4 =$ ___

d. $3 \times 2^2 =$ ___

e. $(25 - 15) + 1 =$ ___

f. $-66 + (2 \times 4^2) \times \frac{1}{2} =$ ___

1. Which two trees are congruent?

2. Solve the problem.

$25\overline{)4095}$

3. The average height of a man is 5 ft, 9 in. A giant sequoia tree can grow up to 50 times that height. How tall can a sequoia grow?

4. All the angles of a quadrilateral must add up to 360°. Find the measure of angle BCD.

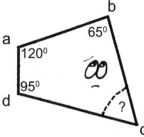

5. Johnson's Garden Center recorded its dogwood tree sales on a plot line for one week during spring planting season. Each tree cost $29.95. How much did the nursery take in for dogwood sales from Monday through Wednesday?

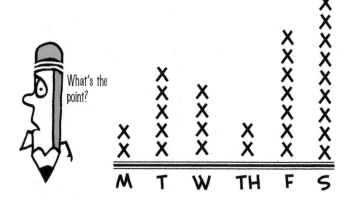

What's the point?

M T W TH F S

1. Solve the problem.   −8 + 3 =
   a. 11   c. −5
   b. −11   d. not here

2. A mature oak tree draws 80 quarts of water out of the earth every day. How many gallons is that?

3. Round each decimal to the nearest tenth.
   a. 59.63 _____
   b. 24.87_____
   c. 39.99_____

4. Find the rule and complete the function table.

   The rule is _____

INPUT	OUTPUT
2	6
3	12
4	20
5	
6	
7	

5. The Burkett kids are avid tree-climbers. Today, after climbing the backyard trees for 4 hours and 42 minutes they took a break from climbing at 12:18 p.m. What time did they start climbing? Show this time on the first watch.

Name

1. Andy solved the problem incorrectly.

12 x 28 = 120

a. What did he forget to do? _____

_____

_____

b. Give the correct answer. _____

2. Which fraction is equivalent to $\frac{3}{5}$?

a. $\frac{9}{12}$ b. $\frac{6}{8}$ c. $\frac{12}{20}$ d. $\frac{13}{15}$

3. Use mental math to solve the problem. This will give you the age of the world's oldest tree, a bristlecone pine.

52 x 100 =

4. Finish the tree to make it symmetrical. Draw a line of symmetry.

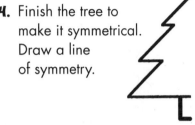

5. Challenge Problem

a. Adam and Abigail (with some help from the neighbors) gathered donations of $600 to plant trees in a corner park. What could they purchase at the Hidden Valley Nursery Spring Sale?

b. It took the neighbors 40 days to raise the money for the trees. The kids decided they wanted to raise more money so they could build a treehouse. If they gathered donations at the same rate, how long would it take them to raise the $990 they need to build the treehouse?

Hidden Valley Nursery Spring Sale

DECIDUOUS	FRUIT	CONIFERS
BEECH......$55.75	APPLE...$125.95	SPRUCE...$150.95
ASPEN......$57.95	PEACH....$75.95	FIR..........$95.95
MAPLE......$65.95	CHERRY..$65.75	PINE........$75.95

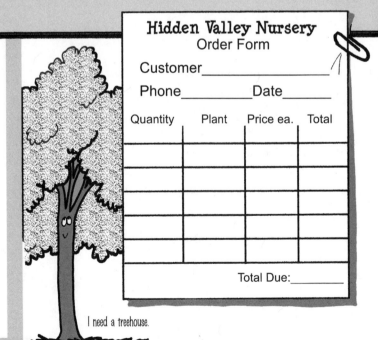

Hidden Valley Nursery
Order Form

Customer_____

Phone_____Date_____

Quantity	Plant	Price ea.	Total
		Total Due:_____	

I need a treehouse.

1. Two-thirds of the 27 ice cream cones served at Hanson's Sweet Shop yesterday had two scoops of ice cream. The rest of the cones all had one scoop. Find the number of . . .

    a. 2-scoop cones _____   b. 1-scoop ones _____

2. Solve the problem. $13\frac{4}{5} - 4\frac{3}{10} =$

3. An ice cream shop owner wants to create a graph showing that ice cream sales increase as the temperature increases. Which kind of graph would work best?

    a. pie   b. line   c. bar   d. picture

4. I'm a space figure with four triangular sides and a square base. What am I?

    a. pyramid   c. rectangular prism

    b. cube   d. triangular prism

Side of each square = 2 cm

5. Pedro decided to create a scale drawing of his giant ice cream cone.

    a. How tall is the actual treat from the bottom tip of the cone to the top?

    b. Estimate the grid area covered by the drawing of the cone.

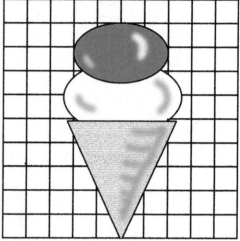

1. Find m if y = 6

    2 y + m = 19

2. Ice cream is best stored at −16°C. The temperature in a faulty freezer is −3°C. How much must the temperature decrease before it will be safe to store ice cream?

3. Round to the nearest whole number and estimate the difference.

    69.3 − 24.9 =

4. Write the standard numeral for three million, two hundred fifteen thousand, one hundred seventy-five.

5. a. Find the cost difference between a quart of Jen and Terrie's Cherry Vanilla ice cream and a quart of Jorden's (same flavor).

    b. What would it cost to buy a quart of each brand?

CHERRY VANILLA ICE CREAM

Jen and Terry's ... $2.83 qt
Freyers' ... $2.78 qt
Jorden's ... $1.99 qt

1. The expression shows an example of the
   _____ property of addition.

   (16 + 8) + 9 = 16 + (8 + 9)

2. Christine will serve double scoop cones at her
   party. The flavor choices will be mint chip, butter
   brickle, vanilla, and strawberry. How many kinds
   of double-scoop cones will her guests have to
   choose from?

3. Twenty-eight percent of the ice cream sold in
   grocery stores in the United States is vanilla.
   A grocery store sells 400 containers of
   ice cream on a certain day. How many
   of them are likely to be vanilla?

4. Find the surface area
   of the ice cream carton.

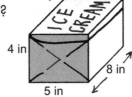

4 in
8 in
5 in

5. Which sundaes are similar?

a
b
c
d
e
g
f

Yummy!

1. Solve the problem.

   $2.4\overline{)7.8}$

2. Find the value of p.

   3p = 36

3. How many cups of liquid are in the recipe?

**FRESH PEACH
ICE CREAM**

$2\frac{2}{3}$ cups heavy cream
$2\frac{1}{2}$ cups light cream
$3\frac{1}{3}$ cups milk
1 cup sugar
2 chopped peaches

I love the way
ice cream tastes.

4. A cup has 8 fluid ounces. How many ounces
   of liquid are in the above recipe?_____

5. Estimate the shaded part of each
   figure using one of these fractions:
   $\frac{1}{2}$, $\frac{1}{4}$, $\frac{2}{5}$, $\frac{2}{3}$, $\frac{1}{3}$, or $\frac{3}{4}$.

   a. _____   b. _____   c. _____

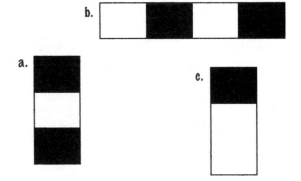

b.

a.

c.

1. If all of your family members eat the average amount of ice cream consumed in the U.S., how many liters will your family consume in one year?

2. How much more ice cream is eaten by the average Australian than by the average Swede in one year?

3. List the countries in order from least to greatest ice cream consumption.

4. The city of Chicago has approximately 200,000 kids ages 10 to14. Assume that each one eats the average amount of ice cream (as shown on the table for U.S.). How many liters of ice cream would Chicago kids in this age range eat in one year?

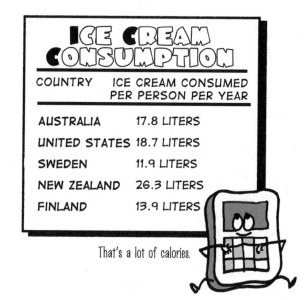

ICE CREAM CONSUMPTION

COUNTRY	ICE CREAM CONSUMED PER PERSON PER YEAR
AUSTRALIA	17.8 LITERS
UNITED STATES	18.7 LITERS
SWEDEN	11.9 LITERS
NEW ZEALAND	26.3 LITERS
FINLAND	13.9 LITERS

That's a lot of calories.

5. Challenge Problem

Arrange the numbers 1–9 in the squares on the banana split so that each of the sides has a sum of **20**.

1. William Penn founded the city of Philadelphia in 1682. The U.S. Constitution was written there in 1774. How old was the city when the Constitution was written?

2. Solve the problem. **24,286 + 9,534 =**

3. Philadelphia covers a total of 135 square miles. What might its dimensions be?

    a. length = 100 mi; width = 35 mi

    b. length = 35 mi; width = 10 mi.

    c. length = 30 mi; width = 4.5 mi

    d. not here

4. Draw a cylinder.

5. Greg spelled the nickname of his favorite city on a cube. (Two views of the cube are shown.) He tosses the cube once. What are his chances of tossing . . .

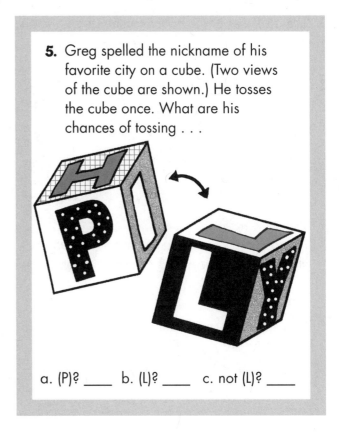

    a. (P)? _____   b. (L)? _____   c. not (L)? _____

1. A Philly cheese steak sandwich at the Reading Station Market costs $6.75. Find the cost of four sandwiches. _____

2. Simplify: **(4r + 6) – r**

    a. 3r + 6

    b. 23r

    c. 4r + (6 – r)

    d. not here

3. Sandy cut 18 inches from a board that measured 2 ft 9 in. How much of the original board was left? _____

4. The population of Philadelphia is **1.5 million**. Write this number in standard form.

Philadelphia Highlights

Independence Hall.....1 hr, 30 min
B. Franklin's Home.............35 min
Betsy Ross's Home........... 45 min
Liberty Bell.................1 hr, 45 min
U.S. Mint.................... 1 hr, 15 min

5. How much time should you schedule if you plan to visit all of the attractions in the brochure (not counting the time it would take to travel between attractions)?

1. The diameter of the bottom of the Liberty Bell is 3 ft 10 inches. Find its circumference.

2. Solve the problem.

$$\frac{3}{5} \div \frac{2}{3} =$$

(Remember to invert the second fraction.)

   a. $\frac{9}{10}$ c. $\frac{2}{5}$
   b. $\frac{6}{10}$ d. not here

Finish the bell of liberty.

3. Philadelphia's annual precipitation is 105 cm. How many **millimeters** of precipitation is this?

   _____

4. Tina spins a 3-section spinner labeled 2, 4, 6. Troy spins a 6-section spinner labeled 2, 4, 6, 8, 10, and 12. Who has a greater chance of spinning a 6? _____

5. Complete the drawing of the Liberty Bell to make its shape symmetrical.

1. Between 1820 and 1860, **eighty thousand** Irish people immigrated to Philadelphia. Write the bold number in exponential form.

2. Solve with $a = 7$.

   $$2a - 1 = \underline{\hspace{2cm}}$$

3. Penn State University has 33,672 students. Write this number in words.

4. What information is missing?

   Dustin bought a T-shirt for $19.95 and a poster for $6.75 at the Philadelphia Museum's gift shop. How much more did he pay for the T-shirt than the puzzle?

   _____

   _____

   _____

5. How many centimeter cubes could you pack into the container?

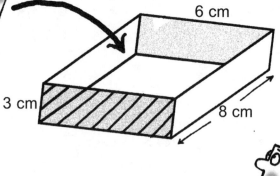

6 cm
3 cm
8 cm

That's a cubic centimeter.

1. Sheri got 18 out of 24 answers correct on her Benjamin Franklin social studies quiz. What was her percentage score? _____

2. Solve the problem.

$$5 - 2\frac{3}{8} =$$

3. Use mental math.

Which of the following numerals can be divided evenly by 3?

5,120   4,217
3,225   1,424

How do you know?

4. About how much would this book weigh?
- a. 1 milliliter
- b. 1 gram
- c. 1 kilogram
- d. 1 milligram

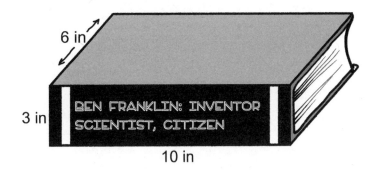

6 in

3 in

BEN FRANKLIN: INVENTOR SCIENTIST, CITIZEN

10 in

5. Challenge Problem

Teryl has twenty-six coins (half dollars, quarters, dimes, nickels, and pennies). The coins total $3.68. How many of each coin might he have? Give two different answers.

Answer #1
_____ half dollars
_____ quarters
_____ dimes
_____ nickels
_____ pennies

Answer #2
_____ half dollars
_____ quarters
_____ dimes
_____ nickels
_____ pennies

.50

.25

The first U.S. Mint was established by Congress in 1792, at Seventh Street and Sugar Alley, in Philadelphia.

1. Clock **a** shows the time a ship *(The Mystic Maid)* began to flounder. She sank one hour and ten minutes later. Show this time on Clock **b**.

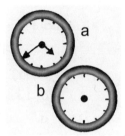

2. **401.02 − 124.6 = 276.42**

   The answer above is ___ correct ___ incorrect

   (If incorrect, give the right answer: _____)

3. Draw a triangle that has three equal sides. What kind of triangle have you drawn? _____

4. Draw the next two ships.

5. Match the term with its definition.

   a. the difference between the smallest and greatest number in a set of numbers   ___range

   b. the average of all the numbers in the set   ___median

   c. the middle number when the numbers are listed in order   ___mode

   d. the number you see the most in the set   ___mean

Ahoy, matey.

1. Of the 2,220 people aboard the *Titanic*, 1,510 died when it sank. Use a calculator to find the percentage of people who didn't survive the shipwreck.

2. Use the number line to solve the problem.

   −10 + 6 = _____

3. Write the lowest terms fraction for $\frac{15}{20}$.

4. Use a protractor to solve the problem.

   A British ship, *The Mary Rose*, sank in 1545. In 1965, divers found it at a _____ - degree angle to the sea floor.

5. Which equation and solution match the statement?

   Add four to my number and multiply by three. The answer is eighteen.

   a. (n x 4) + 3 = 18
       n = 18

   b. (n + 4) x 3 = 18
       n = 2

   c. n + 4 x 3 = 18
       n = 6

   d.   not here

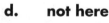

Mary Rose

WEDNESDAY WEEK 28 _____ MATH PRACTICE

1. Cape Horn, off the tip of South America, is a notorious spot for shipwrecks. The air temperature there at 6:00 p.m. was 42°F. By 9:00 p.m., it had dropped 18°F. The 9:00 p.m. temperature was ____° below freezing.

2. Which operation must be completed first?

$$3 \times (6 + 8) + 3 + 2$$

   a. multiply 3 x 6   c. add 6 + 8
   b. add 6 + 8 + 3   d. find the value of 3

3. The ratio of officers to sailors aboard the *Eliza Jane* is 1:15. How many officers are on board if the ship has 75 sailors?

4. Which pair of lines intersects?

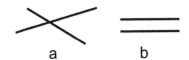

   a   b

5. Write the coordinates for the items retrieved from the sunken ship.

a._____   b._____   c._____

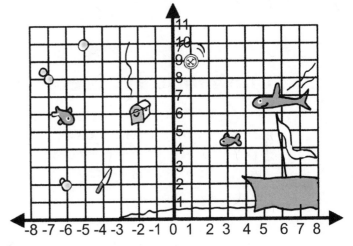

THURSDAY WEEK 28 _____ MATH PRACTICE

1. In 1885, **four hundred million** dollars worth of cargo was retrieved from the sunken ship *The Atocha*. Write the bold number as a standard numeral _____, and as an exponential numeral: 4 x 10.

2. $124 + s = 250$
             $s = 250$

   The answer above is: ___ correct
                          ___ incorrect

   If incorrect,
   give the right answer: _____

3. The remains of an ancient Roman ship were found on the floor the Mediterranean Sea 834 yards below the surface. How deep (in feet) is the sea at the place where the remains were found?

4. Solve the problem. $9 + 0.7 + 3.16 =$

5. A British navy steward, Poon Lim, survived a shipwreck and was alone at sea on a raft from November 23, 1942 until April 5, 1943.

   a. How many days was he at sea before being rescued? _____

   b. About how many months ago did his rescue take place? _____

Use It! Don't Lose It! IP 613-0

1. What is the value of **8** in the numeral **34,286**? _____

2. Round to the hundreds place and estimate the product.

$$698 \times 412 =$$

3. What is the greatest common factor (GCF) of 9 and 27?

4. Josh's library book, **Sunken Treasures**, was due on October 19. It is now December 3 (in the same year). The library charges a $.05 per day late fee. If Josh returns the book today, how much will he have to pay?

5. Challenge Problem

Read the facts about shipwrecks. Find and circle each numeral on the number board. (Numbers may read down, across, or diagonally. Numbers from different items may overlap.)

3	5	2	1	2	8	7	1
9	3	4	0	3	0	8	9
8	0	0	1	3	2	1	0
1	4	1	9	1	4	6	8
6	1	5	8	3	5	2	0
9	6	1	5	9	8	0	3
5	2	0	3	1	0	4	7
3	2	1	2	0	9	2	0
9	7	3	0	1	6	1	6
0	6	4	8	4	8	2	4
2	3	5	6	0	6	7	7
1	0	2	4	0	3	8	1

a. Sable Island, near Nova Scotia, is called the graveyard of the Atlantic because 200 ships have sunk there since the year **one thousand five hundred eighty-three.**

b. A Japanese sea captain and one of his sailors survived adrift at sea for **four hundred eighty-four** days.

c. Archaeologists have found remains of a ship that sank in the year **one thousand four hundred** BC!

d. The *SS Republic* sank off the coast of Georgia while carrying **four hundred thousand dollars** worth of gold.

e. The *Atocha* sank during a hurricane in the year in **one thousand six hundred twenty-two**.

f. To navigate Cape Horn a sea captain must avoid rocks that are **one thousand three hundred ninety-one** meters high.

g. The sunken *Titanic* was located in the year **one thousand nine hundred eighty-five**.

h. The Dutch first navigated Cape Horn, a place of many shipwrecks, in the year **one thousand six hundred sixteen**.

i. When Ernest Shackelton's ship became trapped in an iceberg he and five crew members traveled **one thousand two hundred eighty-seven** kilometers on a lifeboat to find help.

j. With the loss of **one thousand five hundred ten** people, the *Titanic* is one of the worst peacetime disasters.

88

1. A flat-headed frog reaches maturity eight days after its mother lays her eggs. A European frog takes 16 weeks for the same process. How many more **days** does it take for a European frog to develop than a flat-headed frog?

2. Solve the problem.

1586 x 253 =

3. These are Julia's scores on her science quizzes this year. Find the mean.

85, 90, 95, 75, 100

4. Which frogs are congruent?

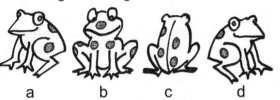

a   b   c   d

5. This is a scale drawing of a Japanese Giant Salamander. What is the actual length of this huge amphibian?

____ inches or ____ feet

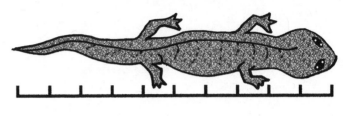

⌐___⌐ = 6 in

1. Find the LCM (lowest common multiple) for the numbers 4, 3, and 8.

2. Estimate the frog's length in centimeters.

_____

Use a ruler to find the actual length to the nearest tenth of a centimeter. _____

3. Solve the problem.

$$\frac{2}{3} \times \frac{3}{5} =$$

Write the answer in lowest terms.

4. **Seven-eighths** of the world's amphibians are frogs. Write this number as a decimal rounded to the nearest hundredth. _____

5. Choose the correct equation. Then solve the problem.

Three times some number plus six equals thirty.

a.   **6q x 3 = 30**
                q =

b.   **3q + 6 = 30**
                q =

c.   **30 – 3q = 6**
                q =

1. Which unit of measurement is best for finding the mass of the toad paperweight?

    a. ounces   c. inches

    b. feet   d. yards

2. Solve the problem.

    $36 \overline{)7711}$

3. You flip a coin 30 times and record the results. About how many times would you expect it to land on heads?_____

4. Name the figures.

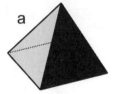 a
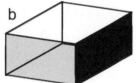 b
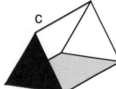 c

5. Isaac made a terrarium for his tree frog science experiment, using the container shown below. He wanted to fill it one-third full of dirt. A bag of dirt covers 500 cubic inches. How many bags would he need to buy?

Home, sweet home.

14 in   20 in   8 in

1. Which operation will make the equation true?

That's not right!

$$45 = (3^4) - (6 \bigcirc 6)$$

    a. addition   c. multiplication

    b. subtraction d. division

2. A frog's heart beats 30 times per minute. At that rate, how many times does it beat . . .

    a. in one hour? ___   b. in one day? ___

3. Place the fractions in order from least to greatest.

    $\frac{3}{4}$ $\frac{2}{3}$ $\frac{7}{8}$

4. What are the next three numerals?

    3, 12, 10, 40, 38, ___, ___, ___

5. Find the difference in the distance covered by the Leapers and the Jumpers.

LEAP FROG CONTEST

Team	Distance Jumped in 30 seconds
Leapers	15 yd, 1 ft, 9 in
Jumpers	14 yd, 2 ft, 11 in

_____ yd

_____ ft

_____ in

1. A female frog lays up to **twenty thousand** eggs at one time. Write the this number as a standard numeral._____

2. Match each angle to its description.

___ acute angle

___ obtuse angle

___ right angle

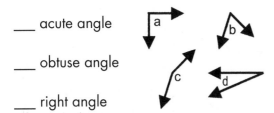

3. Solve the problem.

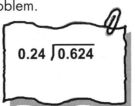

$$0.24 \overline{)0.624}$$

4. A Couch's Spadefoot Toad stays underground 335 days a year. (Pretty boring!) Write a fraction (in lowest terms) to show what part of a year this toad spends underground *(Hint: 365 days = 1 year)*

5. Challenge Problem

You can play with this AMPHIBIAN without getting your hands slimy! Follow these steps:

  a. Cut out the pictures of Scrabble squares.

  b. Set a timer for five minutes.

  c. Make as many words as you can out of the squares.

  d. Write down the words.

  e. Add up the points for each word. Decide if the sum is a prime or composite number.

  f. Keep a record of these words and the points.

  g. Total each column. Is the total a prime or a composite number?

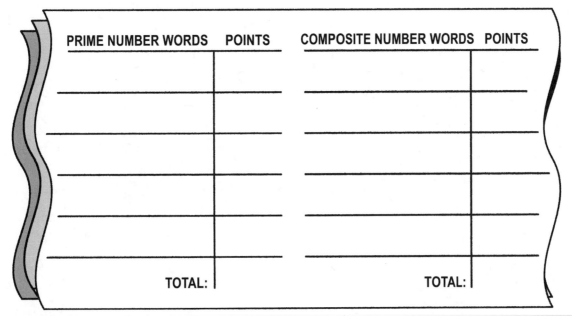

PRIME NUMBER WORDS	POINTS	COMPOSITE NUMBER WORDS	POINTS
TOTAL:		TOTAL:	

1. Find the area of the widescreen TV.

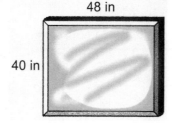

48 in

40 in

2. Email users in North America send an average of **2.7 billion** messages each year. Write this as a standard numeral.

3. Solve the problem.

$$\$29.00 - \$4.89 =$$

4. The first telephone message, sent by its inventor Alexander Graham Bell, was to his assistant:

M R   W A T S O N

a. Which letters have just one line of symmetry?

b. Which letters have more than one?

5. a. How many years passed between the first Morse code message and the first email? _____

b. Was the first telephone call televised to the whole world on the CBS evening news?_____ How can you tell?

Mr. Watson, I need you.

COMMUNICATION FIRSTS	
Event	**Date**
Morse Code Message	1838
Telephone Call	1876
Phone Book	1878
All Electronic TV Program	1927
World-wide Radio Program	1934
E-mail Message	1971

1. Which property is demonstrated?

3,100,000 x 1 = 3,100,000

a. commutative
b. associative
c. distributive
d. property of one

2. Four out of every five Hollywood movie executives believes there is a link between TV violence and real violence. What percentage of executives notices this problem?

3. Simplify the expression: **4d + 5d = 54**

4. Which is a composite number?_____

53   **7**   **83**   **18**   **31**   **17**

5. Find the surface area of this 1934-style radio.

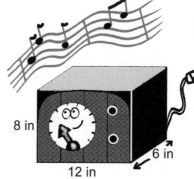

8 in

12 in

6 in

Interesting fact: In 1934, Robert Ripley, a pioneer radio personality, was the first person to broadcast a radio program to every country in the world at the same time.

1. Which cell phones are congruent?

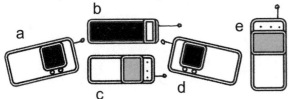

2. Solve the problem.

12 – 15 =

3. Vincent spent 45 minutes on the Internet on Monday. On Tuesday, he spent 15 fewer minutes than on Monday. Wednesday's time was twice as long as Tuesday's, and time on Thursday was twice that of Monday. How much time did he spend on the Internet from Monday through Thursday?

4. A strange radio weather report gave May 7's high temperature as five degrees more than two times thirty. The low temperature was twenty-five degrees less than the high. What were these temperatures?

5. a. Find the difference between Thomasville's high and low temperature on May 3.

b. What pattern do you notice in the Thomasville temperatures for the week of May first?

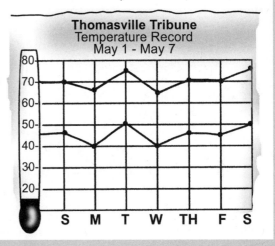

1. Bob Prosser of Turtle Lake, Wisconsin has a collection of **five hundred thousand** telephones. As an exponential number, this is . . .

    a. 50 x 100,000   c. 5×10^{15}

    b. $10^6 \times 5$ d. not here

2. Solve the problem.

5.16 x 3.8 =

3. Grandma Smith prefers to write letters the old-fashioned way with an envelope and stamp. Three-fifths of the 60 letters she sent last winter were by "snail mail." How many letters did she mail with a stamp? _____

4. Solve the problem if w = 15.

(12 + 3) – w = _____

5. Find the difference between the perimeters of the two laptop screens.

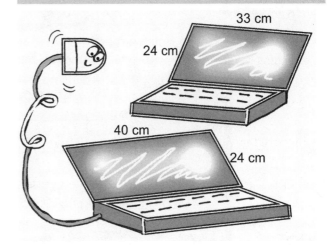

1. Use mental math to solve this problem and find how many Federal Express deliveries are made world-wide every day.

$$200 \times 10{,}000 =$$

2. 520,000,000 pieces of mail are sent every day in the United States! Write the numeral using words. _____

3. Solve the problem.

$$\frac{3}{4} \div \frac{1}{2} =$$

4. Ninety percent of the kids surveyed said they were upset by violence on TV. Two hundred-fifty kids were questioned at Woodrow Elementary. How many were bothered by TV violence? _____

5. Challenge Problem

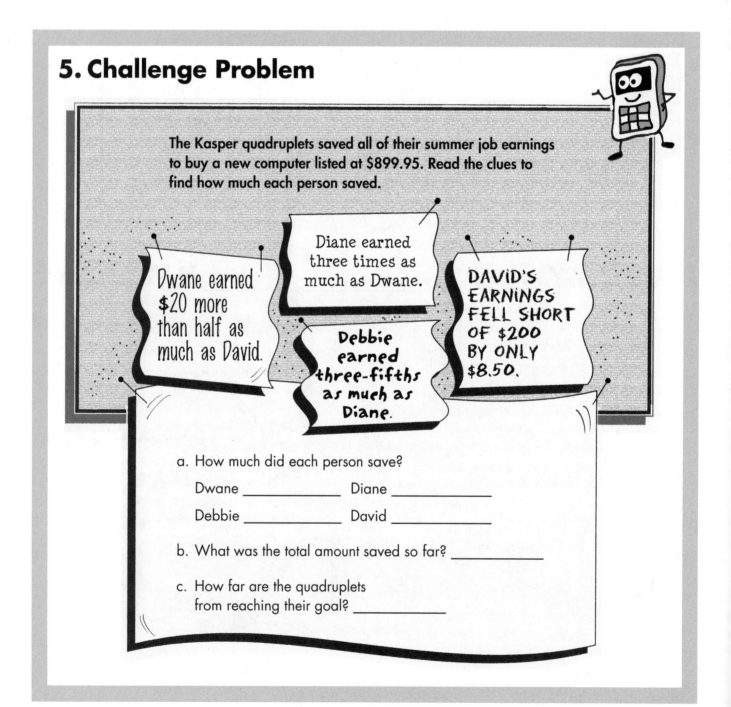

The Kasper quadruplets saved all of their summer job earnings to buy a new computer listed at $899.95. Read the clues to find how much each person saved.

Dwane earned $20 more than half as much as David.

Diane earned three times as much as Dwane.

Debbie earned three-fifths as much as Diane.

DAVID'S EARNINGS FELL SHORT OF $200 BY ONLY $8.50.

a. How much did each person save?

Dwane _____   Diane _____

Debbie _____   David _____

b. What was the total amount saved so far? _____

c. How far are the quadruplets from reaching their goal? _____

1. The Japanese flag is simple and elegant: a large red circle on a plain white background. Find the circumference of the circle if its diameter is 12 inches.

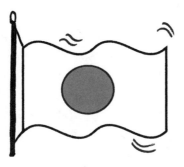

2. Subtract to solve. Add in reverse to check.

8023 – 1641 =

3. A Japanese elementary school has one teacher for every 20 students. At this rate, how many teachers are there for 220 students?

4. Which is not a parallelogram? How do you know?

 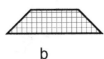

a   b   c   d

5. List the possible outcomes of spinning each spinner once.

a. There are ____ possible outcomes.

b. The chances of spinning a 2 and sushi are _____.

I vote for sushi.

1. Which solution is correct?

3p + 5 = 14

a. p = 8   c. p = 6
b. p = 9   d. p = 3

2. Mr. Trent's class was watching a $1\frac{1}{2}$-hour movie called *Growing Up in Japan* when the DVD player broke down halfway through the movie. How many minutes had the class watched before the player broke?

3. Place the decimals in order from least to greatest.
0.14   1.14   1.4   0.014   0.04

4. Tokyo, Japan has pleasant summers and cool winters. What is the range between its winter and summer temperatures?

Average Temperatures in Tokyo	
Winter	41° F
Summer	77° F

5. Round each number to the hundreds place and estimate the sum.

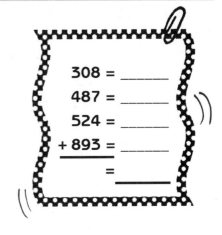

308 = _____
487 = _____
524 = _____
+ 893 = _____
= _____

1. Sumo wrestling is an ancient Japanese martial art. The largest sumo wrestler, Chad Rowa, weighs 228 kg. How many pounds does he weigh? _____ (Hint: 1 kg = 2.2 lb)

2.
18.1 – 12.63 = 5.53

The solution is __ correct __ incorrect.

3. What information is **not** needed to solve the problem?

Every year about 6.1 million tourists visit Japan and spend an average of $11.3 billion dollars during their stay. How many visitors will travel to Japan in the next four years?

4. Study the pieces of the tangram puzzle.
   a. How many triangles?
   b. How many parallelograms?
   c. How many squares?

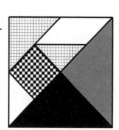

5. With your eyes closed, you will pick up two of these Dominoes. Then you will add all of the dots. What are your chances of having a sum greater than 10?

1. What is the next number in the pattern?

1, 5, 25, 125, _____

2. Miyu invited seven friends for a traditional Japanese tea ceremony. She's preparing 6 ounces of tea for each person at the ceremony. How many ounces of tea should she make? _____

3. Round each to the nearest hundredth.
   a. 4.012 = _____   b. 0.529 = _____
        c. 0.008 = _____

4. List the steps for solving this correctly.
   4 + (6 x 3) – 1 =

   a.

   b.

   c.

5. Eleven year-old Sadako, her fifteen year-old brother, and two parents had dinner at the sushi bar. Find the cost of their dinner.

WEDNESDAY SUSHI SPECIAL ALL YOU CAN EAT

Adults $8.95
Children (under 12) $5.95

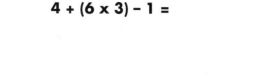

Name

1. Ren attends cram classes for 1 hour 15 minutes each night Monday to Friday and 2 hours on Saturday. How much time does he spend in cram classes each week? _____

2. Solve the problem.

Interesting Fact: Japanese children often attend "cram" school after their regular school day to prepare for difficult exams.

$$2\frac{2}{5} + 3\frac{2}{3} = \underline{\quad}$$

3. Kagoshima, Japan gets **88** inches of rain each year. Write this number as ____ yd, ____ ft, ____ in

4. An art teacher will cut an 18 by 48-inch piece of white paper into 6-inch squares for teaching an Origami lesson. How many 6 inch squares can be cut from the large sheet of paper? _____

5. Challenge Problem

Solve the Japanese Sudoku puzzle. Use each of the numbers 1–9 once in each row and column to fill in the blanks. No number may appear more than once in any row, column, or small nine-square box.

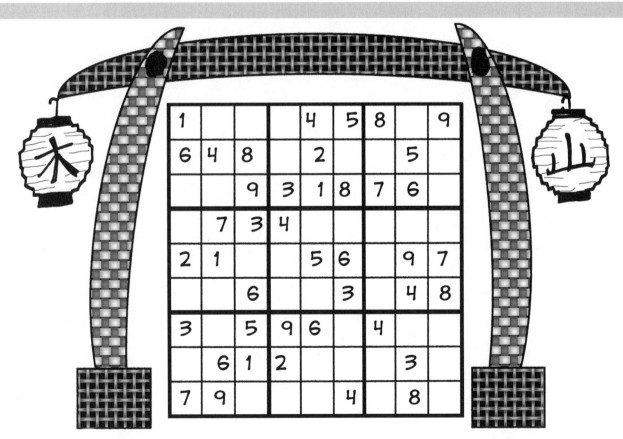

1				4		5	8		9
6	4	8		2				5	
		9	3	1	8	7	6		
	7	3	4						
2	1			5	6		9	7	
	6				3		4	8	
3		5	9	6		4			
	6	1	2				3		
7	9				4		8		

1. In 2004 the Boston Red Sox beat the St. Louis Cardinals in a four-game sweep and won the World Series. It was their first World Series win in 86 years. When was the last time the Sox won the world championship before 2004?

2. Solve the problem.

$$536 \times 424 =$$

3. Sixty-five percent of the voters of Littletown, Arkansas wanted to install lights in their baseball stadium. There are 5,260 eligible voters in Littletown. How many voted to light up the stadium?

4. Define *trapezoid*. _____
_____
_____

Draw one.

5. What words should be written in the shared part of the Venn diagram?

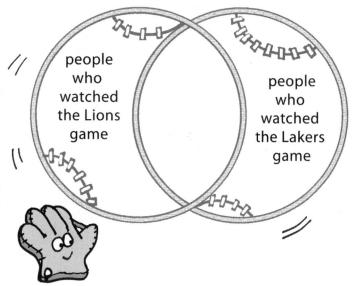

1. Solve the problem to find the number of years that Nolan Ryan played professional baseball: (b = 12).

$$3b - 9 =$$

2. Write each fraction in lowest terms.

a. $\frac{9}{27}$ _____   b. $\frac{12}{16}$ _____   c. $\frac{5}{20}$ _____

3. A regulation baseball is 9 inches or about _____ cm in circumference.

4. Which sign makes the expression true?

$$(27 \bigcirc 9) + (24 \div 3) = 11$$

a. +   c. x
b. −   d. ÷

Thwack!

5. Find the area of a baseball diamond . . .
   a. in square feet _____
   b. Change your answer into square yards. _____

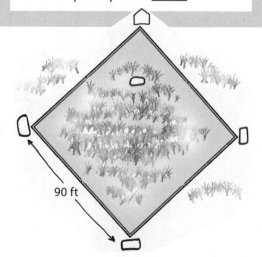

90 ft

1. The Whackers scored the following number of runs in their first five games: 6, 4, 8, 3, 9. Find the mean of this data. _____

2. Solve the problem.

$$6 - 14 =$$

3. Use mental math to solve.

Cy Young has the most wins (511) and the most losses (316) of any major league baseball player. How many games does that represent? _____

4. Estimate the width of the pictured mitt in centimeters. _____ cm

Measure. How close was your estimate?
_____ cm

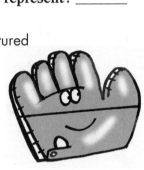

5. Write the ordered pair that shows the location of each of these:

baseball mitt _____   baseball bat _____

batting helmet _____   home plate _____

1. Mickey Mantle hit a **643**-foot homer in Detroit in 1960 and holds the record for the longest ever-recorded home run. Write the bold numeral in expanded form.

2. Solve the problem.

$$0.12 \overline{)0.672}$$

3. Find **v** if m = 16.

$$m - v = 9$$

4. Use the scale drawing to find the maximum length of a regulation-size baseball bat.

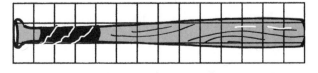

☐ = 3 in

5. Ellie has $6.50 to spend on lunch following Saturday's Babe Ruth game. List two lunches she might choose. Find the total for each.

Snack Bar

Hot dog.........$2.50
Chili dog........$3.00
Burger............$3.50
Double
    Burger.......$4.25
Fries................$1.75
Nachos...........$2.25
Drinks....Sm. .$0.85
          Med. .$1.00
          Lg. .$1.50

Name

1. The New York Yankees won 26 of the 39 World Series championships they played in. Find the percentage of the series they won. Round your answer to the nearest whole percent. _____

2. Solve. Write the answer in lowest terms.

$$3\frac{2}{7} \times 1\frac{2}{3} =$$

5. Challenge Problem

Make a pie graph that accurately communicates the number of Little League World Series wins for each of the countries in the table.

Little League World Series Winners

U.S._____	29
Mexico_____	3
Japan_____	6
Taiwan____	17
S. Korea___	2
Venezuela___	2
Curacao____	1

3. There are 56 boys and 52 girls in the baseball league this year. Each team will have 12 players. How many teams? _____

4. Cal Ripken played more consecutive career games (over 2,600) than any other pro baseball player. Write the numeral in words.

1. Which two skyscrapers are congruent?

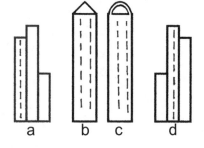

a   b   c   d

2. Use mental math to solve:

40,000 x 1000 = _____

3. The chances that it will rain during the week of June 3rd are 2 out of 7. What does that mean?

4. You'll be in Chicago for a short time and want to tour two of these famous buildings. List all the possible combinations of two buildings.

CHICAGO HIGHLIGHTS

SEARS TOWER & SKY DECK

JOHN HANCOCK OBSERVATORY

FIELD MUSEUM OF NATURAL HISTORY

AON CENTER

5. The tallest office building in the United Kingdom is 1 Canada Square in London. Use a protractor to measure the number of degrees in the peak of the roof.

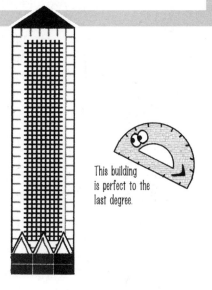

This building is perfect to the last degree.

1. The first U.S. skyscraper was built in Chicago in 1885. How many decades ago was this?

2. Round each fractional number to the nearest whole number.

a. $3\frac{1}{5}$ b. $4\frac{2}{3}$ c. $6\frac{7}{8}$

3. Which property is shown in this expression?

p x q = q x p

a. associative   c. zero
b. distributive   d. commutative

4. Which angle is closest to 50°?

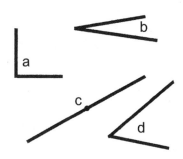

What a towering feat!

5. Which equation can be used to solve the problem?

The Chrysler Building, which is 1,046 feet tall, is six feet shorter than the Eiffel Tower. How tall is the Eiffel Tower?

a. 1046 – 6 = _____

b. 6 x 1046 = _____

c. 6 + 1046 = _____

d. 1046 ÷ _____ = 6

WEDNESDAY WEEK 33 _____ MATH PRACTICE

1. The Empire State Building is struck by lightning about 100 times a year. At that rate, about how many times has it been struck since its completion in 1931?

2. Solve the problem. $2\frac{3}{8} \div \frac{3}{4} =$
(Write the answer in lowest terms.)

3. A group arrives at the top of the Empire State Building at 10:45 a.m. After spending 45 minutes at the observation deck, they take a 5-minute elevator ride to the ground floor. What time will they get off the elevator?

4. a. Draw an acute angle. Label it A.
   b. Draw an obtuse angle. Label it O.

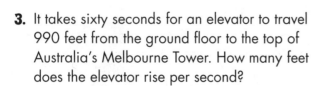

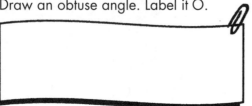

| X = 5 STUDENTS |

Not again!

Chrysler Building | Sears Tower | Eiffel Tower | Empire State Building

5. The plot line graph shows data from a survey asking, "Which building would you most like to visit?"
   a. How many students took part in the survey?
   b. How many more wanted to visit the Empire State Building than the Chrysler Building?

THURSDAY WEEK 33 _____ MATH PRACTICE

1. The Amoco Building has **80** stories and the Woolworth Building has **60** stories. What is the Greatest Common Factor (GCF) of these two numbers?

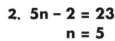

Figure it out!

2. **5n − 2 = 23**
   n = 5

   This solution is ___correct ___incorrect.
   (If incorrect, give the right answer.)

3. It takes sixty seconds for an elevator to travel 990 feet from the ground floor to the top of Australia's Melbourne Tower. How many feet does the elevator rise per second?

4. Solve the problem.

   19.2 x 0.24 =

5. How many cubes were used to build this model skyscraper?

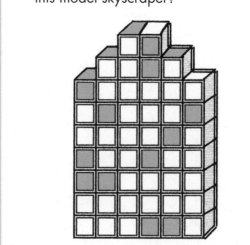

Name

1. Which of the following can be evenly divided by 5?

4,128   2,343   5,025   1,680

How can you tell?_____

2. The CN Tower in Toronto, Canada is 1815 feet tall. What is the value of the 8 in this number?

3. Tell whether each statement is true or false:

___ a. 18.6 = 12.3 + 6.3

___ b. 2.16 – 0.09 = 2.70

4. Sam gives the clerk $15.00 for a poster with a price of $10.85. How much change would he get?

I fell for the "Eifell" tower.

$10.85

5. Challenge Problem

DESIGN YOUR OWN SKYSCRAPER

1. Cut a 6 x 3-inch rectangle out of black paper.

2. Fold the paper in half lengthwise.

3. Use white crayon or light pencil to sketch one side of a skyscraper that fills the paper top to bottom.

4. Leaving the paper folded, cut along your sketch line.

5. Make sure you do not cut on the fold.

6. Unfold. Your building should be symmetrical.

7. Glue or tape it to the grid.

8. Create a reasonable scale for a skyscraper. *One square = _____ feet²*.

9. How tall would your actual skyscraper be? _____

1. Twelve percent of the world's horses live in the United States. There are 60,000,000 horses worldwide. How many are located in the U.S.?

2. Solve the problem.

$$12\frac{3}{10} - 4\frac{4}{5} =$$

3. Karla trains her horse every day after school. The time she spent last week was as follows: Monday: 55 min, Tuesday: 45 min, Wednesday: 35 min, Thursday: 50 min, Friday: 1 hr. What is the average time she spent training each day?

4. Find the circumference of the horse training ring.

21 ft

5. Draw . . .
- a pair of perpendicular lines (label A)
- a pair of parallel lines (label B)
- a pair of intersecting lines that are perpendicular (label C)
- a pair of intersecting lines that are not perpendicular (label D)

1. A male horse has 40 teeth and a female has 36. Find the greatest common factor of the two numbers.

2. Which operation would you do first?

$$3 \times 10^2 + (5 \times 6) =$$

a. multiply 5 x 6
b. find the value of 10^2
c. multiply 3×10^2

3. Flash, a young filly, weighs 372 kg. The vet says she'll probably weigh 425 kg when she's an adult. How much weight will she gain by the time she's full grown?

4. Shade the next figure in the pattern. Then write a fraction to describe the shaded part.

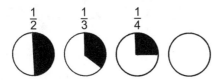

$\frac{1}{2}$ $\frac{1}{3}$ $\frac{1}{4}$

5. Which unit of measurement would you use to weigh the bale of hay?

a. gram
b. ton
c. ounce
d. milligram
e. none of these

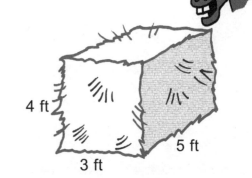

4 ft
3 ft
5 ft

1. Solve the problem.

$$-8 + 7 =$$

   a. 15   b. –1   c. –15   d. not here

2. The temperature was 54°F at 6:30 a.m. when the riders mounted their horses. By 12:00 p.m. it had risen to 82°F. Find the increase in the temperature between 6:30 a.m. and noon.

3. Write the next three numerals to follow the pattern: 1, 1, 2, 6, 24, _____, _____, _____

4. Name the figures.

   a._____   b. _____   c. _____

5. The graph records the number of times each of these books was checked out in a year.

   a. What is the difference between the number of checkouts for *Seabiscuit* and *Wild Horse Running*?

   b. Can the graph be used to find the total number of students who checked out horse books? _____. Explain.

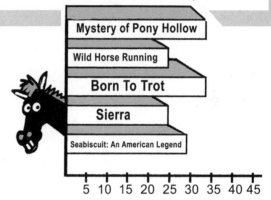

1. Find the value of **p** if **r** = 18.

$$r - 2p = 8$$
$$p = \underline{\hspace{1cm}}$$

2. Of the 400 horses recommended for the Kentucky Derby each year, only 20 are chosen for the race. Write a fraction (in lowest terms) that compares the number chosen to the number recommended.

3. Solve the problem.

$$2\frac{3}{10} \times 1\frac{1}{2} =$$

4. The saddle in #5 weighs 15.9 kg. UPS wants to know its weight in pounds so they can calculate the delivery fee.

   15.9 kg = _____ lb

(Hint: 1 kg = 2.2 pounds)

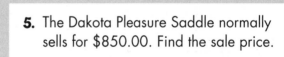

I'm wearing my Kentucky derby.

5. The Dakota Pleasure Saddle normally sells for $850.00. Find the sale price.

Saddle Sale

25% OFF

Tues - Thurs. Only

THOROUGHBRED TRIVIA

1. Cigar, with a total of 10^7 has earned more than any other thoroughbred. How much is this?

2. The United States has won $23 \overline{)1058}$ medals in Olympic Equestrian events. How many is this?

3. Secretariat ran the Kentucky Derby in 119 seconds and set a record for the fastest time ever. This is _____ min _____ sec.

4. Aristides won the very first Kentucky Derby in 1000 + 800 + 70 + 5. What year is this?

5. Challenge Problem

John wants to reseed his pasture with alfalfa seeds to provide great feed for his horses. Each bag of seed covers 350 square meters.

a. What is the area of his pasture?_____

b. How many bags of seed does he need to purchase? _____

c. If each bag costs $37.95, how much will he spend? _____

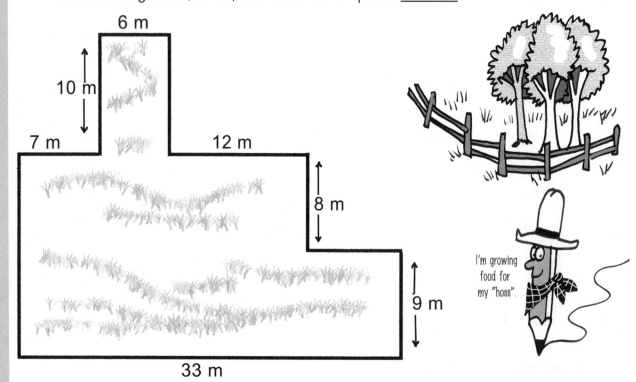

I'm growing food for my "hoss".

1. The area of Crater Lake is 20 square miles. The lake is 6 miles wide. About how many miles long is the lake?

    a. 120   c. 14

    b. 3.3   d. not here

2. Round each number to the greatest place value and estimate the product.

    313 x 482 =

3. Zack and Zeke will walk around Crater Lake at a rate of 3.2 miles per hour. How much distance will they cover during their three-hour hike?

4. Which hiking boots are similar?

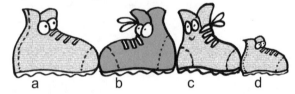

  a   b   c   d

5. A group of hikers is preparing for a walk at Crater Lake. The leader has asked everyone to bring the following: a sweater or jacket, a granola bar or piece of fruit, and a container of orange juice or water.

Draw a tree diagram to see how many possible combinations of supplies the hikers can bring.

1. Use mental math to solve the problem.

    Crater Lake was discovered by prospectors who named it Deep Blue Lake in 1853. Its name was changed to Crater Lake in 1869. How long did the lake have its original name?

2. Find the Least Common Multiple (LCM) for 5 and 6.

3. With a depth of 1,932 feet, Crater Lake is the deepest lake in the United States. Find the depth of the lake in yards.

4. Place the numbers 1, 2, 3, 4 in the fraction boxes so they add up to the given sum.

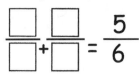

I'm thinking of a number. If I add 7 to it and multiply the sum by 4, my answer will be 40. What's my number?

5. a. Circle the equation that can be used to find the number.

    40 = (4 + 7) x n   (n + 7) x 4 = 40

    b. Find the value of n. _____

1. How many degrees are in angle ABC?

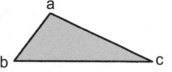

2. Solve the problem. Draw a number line to check your answer.

$$-1 + -8 =$$

3. Find the product:

$$1,524 \times 36 =$$

4. The Bedford family will draw one card from each pile to decide how they will spend the first of their three days in southern Oregon. What are the chances that they will go to Crater Lake on Monday?

5. Use the scale to find the actual height of Wizard Island.

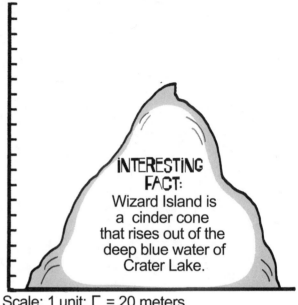

INTERESTING FACT: Wizard Island is a cinder cone that rises out of the deep blue water of Crater Lake.

Scale: 1 unit; ⊏ = 20 meters

1. Compare the fractions. Add **<**, **>**, or **=**.

$$\frac{4}{5} \bigcirc \frac{5}{6}$$

2. Some hikers began their descent from the rim of Crater Lake to the water's edge at 11:23 a.m. and arrived in time for a noon picnic. How long did the hike take?

3. Is the answer correct? _____

$$6m + 5 = 23$$
$$m = 4$$

If not, what is the correct answer?_____

4. Which sign makes the expression true?

$$3 + (4 \bigcirc 8) = 35$$

a. +   b. –   c. x   d. ÷

What's a good time for lunch?

5. A delivery service left a crate of cinnamon roll dough at the back door of the Crater Lake Lodge's kitchen. Four hungry bears got to the box before the cook found it. The dough completely filled the box. Each bear ate a paw full of dough measuring 4 x 4 x 6 inches. Did the bears eat all the dough in the box?

24 in

10 in

12 in

1. Order the numerals from least to greatest.

1.2   0.12   0.012   10.2   0.112

2. Solve the problem.

$$25\frac{7}{10} - 2\frac{3}{5} =$$

3. Circle each composite number. Draw a box around each prime number.

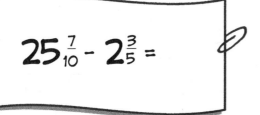

24   11   17   14   3   21   2

4. Use mental math to solve:

32,000 ÷ 100 =

5. Challenge Problem

Seventy-five eager tourists piled onto the bus for a breathtaking tour of Crater Lake. One-third of the passengers were seniors, two-fifths were adults, twenty percent were kids 5–17, and the rest were children under five.

All aboard!

Crater Lake Special

CRATER LAKE BUS TOURS

Seniors..........................$15.75

Adults 18 and over......................$20.00

Children 5-17 ....$12.50

Children under 5......................$5.75

a. How many people in each age group were on the bus?

Seniors........ _____

Adults .... _____

Kids 5–17 ... _____

Under 5 ...... _____

b. How much fare did the bus company collect from the tourists? _____

1. The first people to use fireworks for celebrations were the Chinese in the early 800s. For **about** how many years have people used fireworks?

2. Solve the problem.

$$3.1 + 2.75 + 0.15 =$$

3. To celebrate Independence Day and earn a Guinness record, Frank Dellaros ate 21 hotdogs in 12 minutes. How many seconds did it take to eat each hotdog?

4. This fireworks design is symmetrical. Draw the rest of the picture.

USE A CRAYON.

5. The Bayside Inn hosts many celebrations. During the summer of 2006, wedding receptions were the most frequent occasions at this site. There were thirty-two in June, thirty-five in July, thirty-eight in August, and thirty-one in September. Make a table to organize this data.

1. Every day **six hundred million seventy three thousand six hundred ninety-three** people celebrate their birthdays in the U.S. Write this number in standard form.

2. Simplify; then find the value of v.

$$3v + 2v = 50$$

3. Solve the problem.

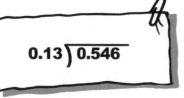

$$0.13 \overline{)0.546}$$

4. So many people get married in Las Vegas, Nevada that there's a wedding every five minutes. At that rate, how many people get married . . .

    a. in an hour? _____

    b. in a day? _____

5. Find the surface area of the present.

Don't shake me!

15 in

8 in

12 in

1. A royal wedding took place in London on July 29, 1981. Seven hundred fifty thousand people watched it on TV, 250,000 listened on the radio and 500,000 lined the streets to watch it live. How many people witnessed the wedding in some way?

2. What property is shown in this example?

   31 x 6 = (30 x 6) + (1 x 6)

3. Five members of one family will celebrate their birthdays in June. Jamie will turn 3, Pete 10, Hillary 16, Mom 39, and Grandpa 64. What type of a graph best compares the ages of the birthday folks?

4. **Estimate** the length of the candle, to the nearest centimeter, from the tip of the flame to the bottom. **Measure** to check your estimate.

   Estimate: _____ cm   Actual: _____ cm

5. Read the passage.

   Draw the following party items at these locations: party hat (2, 4); wrapped gift (4, 5); balloon (–3, 4); party noisemaker (–2, 2); ice cream cone (–4, 0); balloon (0, 4)

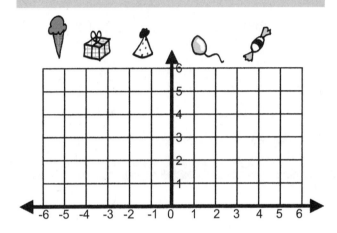

1. Is the solution accurate?

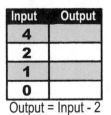

$$24\overline{)820} \quad 34\ r\ 4$$

2. Nine of the twelve cake orders at Fritches Bakery last Saturday were for birthday parties. Write a fraction (in lowest terms) that compares the number of birthday cakes to the total number of cakes ordered.

3. The cake in problem #5 will be cut into 3″ x 3″ x 3″ servings. How many people will the cake serve?

4. Complete the function table for the given rule.

Input	Output
4	
2	
1	
0	

Output = Input - 2

5. The top edge of the graduation cake will be decorated with miniature frosting roses placed side by side. Each rose is $\frac{1}{2}$ inch wide. How many roses are needed?

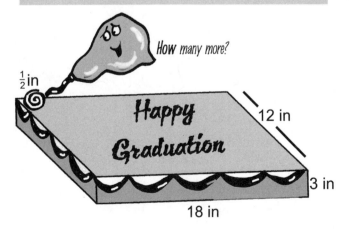

How many more?

$\frac{1}{2}$ in   12 in

Happy Graduation

3 in

18 in

Fourth of July in Brighton

Parade	9:15 am – 10:45 am
Craft Fair	11:00 am – 2:30 pm
Elks Club BBQ	12:00 pm – 2:00 pm
Chicken Dinner	

Adults	$ 7.95
Kids under 12	$ 3.95

Antique Car Show	3:30 pm
Band Concert	4:30 pm
Lakeside Fireworks	8:45 pm

1. Find the cost of two adult and three child BBQ chicken dinners.

2. About how many hours will pass between the end of the parade and the beginning of the band concert?

3. The ratio of children who will ride on floats to adults is 4:1. Thirty-five adults will ride on floats. How many children will ride?

4. The Elks Club will serve an 8-ounce glass of lemonade with every BBQ chicken dinner. The cooks expect to sell 250 dinners. How many **gallons** of lemonade should they prepare? _____
(Hint: 1 gallon = 128 ounces)

5. Challenge Problem

The Sidewalk Café served 74 ice cream cones between noon and 1:30 p.m. on the Fourth of July. Some were single, some were double, and some were triple scoops. One hundred thirty-eight scoops of ice cream were served. How many of the cones were single, how many were double, and how many were triple scoops?

single _____

double _____

triple _____

We're having an ice cream party!

Ooops!

INCENTIVE PUBLICATIONS DAILY PRACTICE SERIES
GRADE 5 MATH SKILLS

Number Concepts

Skill	1	2	3	4	5	6	7	8	9	10	11	12	13	14	15	16	17	18	19	20	21	22	23	24	25	26	27	28	29	30	31	32	33	34	35	36
Whole numbers: read, write, compare, order	✓			✓		✓			✓	✓				✓		✓	✓	✓		✓	✓	✓	✓	✓			✓	✓		✓	✓					✓
Whole numbers: prime and composite numbers				✓			✓						✓										✓					✓	✓						✓	
Whole numbers: place value			✓	✓	✓					✓			✓	✓		✓		✓			✓		✓					✓						✓		
Whole numbers: rounding	✓					✓		✓								✓		✓	✓			✓		✓					✓	✓			✓			✓
Multiples, CM, LCM												✓		✓					✓		✓	✓							✓							
Factors, CF, GCF	✓		✓						✓	✓					✓					✓				✓				✓					✓			
Divisibility				✓															✓	✓	✓						✓									
Exponential numbers						✓			✓		✓			✓	✓			✓		✓	✓	✓	✓		✓		✓	✓						✓		
Fractions: read, write, compare, order		✓								✓	✓							✓				✓				✓					✓					
Fractions: rounding								✓									✓								✓					✓						
Equivalent fractions		✓				✓	✓		✓				✓			✓		✓			✓				✓	✓			✓			✓				
Fractions in lowest terms	✓	✓			✓			✓			✓	✓	✓	✓	✓				✓	✓		✓	✓	✓	✓		✓	✓	✓		✓	✓	✓			
Ratios					✓										✓			✓				✓								✓						
Decimals: read, write, compare, order		✓				✓				✓			✓					✓			✓					✓	✓			✓	✓	✓				
Decimals: rounding			✓				✓												✓					✓		✓	✓		✓		✓					
Percent			✓		✓				✓					✓						✓			✓	✓					✓			✓			✓	
Fractions, decimals, percent relationships		✓										✓		✓					✓			✓				✓	✓	✓	✓	✓	✓	✓		✓	✓	
Money	✓		✓		✓		✓			✓				✓	✓				✓		✓				✓			✓	✓	✓	✓	✓			✓	✓

Use It! Don't Lose It! IP 613-0

INCENTIVE PUBLICATIONS DAILY PRACTICE SERIES
GRADE 5 MATH SKILLS

Operations/Computations

Skill	1	2	3	4	5	6	7	8	9	10	11	12	13	14	15	16	17	18	19	20	21	22	23	24	25	26	27	28	29	30	31	32	33	34	35	36
Properties		✓																					✓			✓				✓			✓			✓
Order of operations			✓			✓					✓	✓					✓			✓		✓		✓			✓				✓			✓		
Add and subtract whole numbers	✓		✓	✓	✓					✓	✓		✓	✓	✓		✓	✓	✓	✓	✓				✓		✓	✓			✓	✓			✓	
Multiply whole numbers		✓		✓		✓			✓					✓			✓		✓	✓		✓							✓				✓		✓	
Divide whole numbers			✓		✓	✓			✓	✓		✓	✓	✓	✓	✓	✓						✓		✓		✓				✓	✓				✓
Multiply and divide with multiples of 10			✓						✓						✓	✓					✓							✓							✓	
Averages	✓	✓	✓				✓	✓		✓				✓		✓	✓									✓			✓			✓				
Add and subtract fractions		✓		✓	✓						✓		✓					✓	✓	✓		✓	✓			✓	✓		✓	✓	✓			✓		
Multiply fractions		✓	✓		✓				✓			✓	✓				✓	✓			✓			✓		✓						✓	✓	✓		
Divide fractions																✓			✓					✓			✓			✓			✓			
Add and subtract decimals		✓	✓		✓	✓		✓	✓	✓	✓	✓	✓		✓	✓	✓	✓	✓	✓	✓	✓		✓	✓	✓		✓	✓		✓	✓			✓	✓
Multiply decimals			✓						✓	✓			✓	✓	✓		✓				✓	✓	✓			✓	✓							✓		
Divide decimals							✓															✓						✓		✓				✓			✓
Operations with money		✓	✓		✓	✓		✓	✓	✓	✓	✓	✓	✓	✓	✓		✓	✓	✓	✓	✓	✓	✓	✓	✓	✓		✓	✓	✓	✓			✓	
Add integers	✓	✓						✓		✓	✓		✓	✓	✓	✓	✓	✓	✓	✓		✓	✓			✓	✓	✓	✓			✓		✓	✓	
Subtract integers	✓			✓	✓	✓		✓			✓		✓	✓	✓	✓	✓	✓				✓	✓		✓			✓	✓				✓	✓		
Estimate answers																														✓	✓	✓	✓	✓	✓	✓
Find missing operation				✓						✓			✓	✓			✓		✓						✓			✓			✓				✓	
Verify accuracy of computations		✓	✓	✓	✓									✓	✓	✓	✓					✓			✓						✓	✓			✓	✓

114

© Incentive Publications, Inc. Nashville, TN

INCENTIVE PUBLICATIONS DAILY PRACTICE SERIES
GRADE 5 MATH SKILLS

Problem Solving

Skill	1	2	3	4	5	6	7	8	9	10	11	12	13	14	15	16	17	18	19	20	21	22	23	24	25	26	27	28	29	30	31	32	33	34	35	36
Identify problem	✓	✓	✓			✓	✓		✓	✓	✓	✓	✓	✓	✓	✓	✓	✓	✓	✓	✓	✓	✓	✓	✓	✓		✓	✓	✓	✓	✓	✓	✓		
Necessary information	✓			✓		✓	✓	✓	✓	✓	✓	✓	✓	✓	✓	✓	✓	✓	✓	✓	✓	✓	✓		✓	✓	✓	✓	✓	✓	✓	✓	✓	✓		
Necessary operations; order of operations			✓	✓					✓		✓		✓	✓		✓	✓	✓	✓	✓	✓	✓	✓	✓	✓	✓		✓	✓	✓	✓	✓				✓
Choose strategy		✓		✓			✓	✓		✓					✓		✓		✓	✓		✓	✓		✓	✓			✓			✓	✓	✓		✓
Translate into an equation			✓	✓	✓	✓		✓	✓	✓	✓	✓	✓	✓	✓	✓	✓	✓	✓	✓	✓	✓	✓	✓	✓	✓			✓		✓	✓	✓			✓
Complete or extend a pattern	✓		✓	✓			✓		✓				✓	✓		✓			✓		✓		✓					✓		✓	✓			✓		
Use a formula	✓					✓		✓		✓					✓		✓		✓		✓	✓			✓	✓										✓
Use diagrams/illustrations	·	✓	✓	✓	✓	✓	✓	✓	✓	✓		✓		✓	✓	✓	✓	✓	✓		✓	✓			✓	✓	✓			✓		✓				✓
Use estimation	✓	✓	✓		✓	✓	✓	✓	✓	✓	✓	✓	✓		✓			✓		✓		✓	✓	✓	✓	✓	✓		✓	✓	✓	✓				✓
Use mental math		✓													✓		✓						✓	✓		✓	✓		✓	✓		✓			✓	
Use logic					✓		✓	✓		✓		✓	✓	✓	✓	✓	✓	✓	✓	✓	✓	✓	✓	✓	✓	✓	✓	✓	✓	✓	✓	✓	✓			
Use trial and error	✓			✓				✓	✓	✓	✓	✓		✓	✓	✓		✓	✓		✓		✓		✓	✓	✓	✓	✓	✓		✓		✓	✓	✓
Use a graph or table	✓	✓	✓		✓	✓	✓	✓	✓	✓	✓	✓	✓	✓	✓	✓	✓	✓				✓		✓	✓	✓				✓				✓		✓
Problems w/ whole numbers	✓	✓	✓	✓	✓	✓	✓	✓	✓	✓	✓	✓	✓	✓	✓	✓	✓	✓	✓	✓	✓	✓		✓	✓	✓	✓	✓	✓	✓	✓	✓	✓	✓	✓	✓
Problems w/ fractions	✓			✓	✓				✓				✓	✓								✓			✓				✓	✓	✓					
Problems w/ decimals		✓	✓	✓						✓	✓								✓	✓	✓	✓	✓	✓	✓		✓	✓	✓					✓		
Problems w/ percent				✓	✓		✓			✓		✓			✓			✓		✓		✓	✓		✓	✓	✓	✓	✓	✓	✓			✓		
Problems w/ positive and negative numbers								✓										✓				✓				✓					✓					
Problems w/ rate or ratio	✓				✓	✓	✓	✓	✓	✓	✓	✓	✓	✓	✓	✓	✓	✓	✓	✓	✓	✓	✓	✓	✓	✓	✓	✓	✓	✓	✓	✓		✓	✓	✓
Problems w/ money	✓	✓	✓	✓		✓	✓	✓	✓	✓		✓	✓		✓	✓	✓		✓	✓	✓	✓	✓	✓	✓	✓	✓	✓		✓	✓	✓		✓		✓
Problems w/ time	✓	✓	✓	✓	✓	✓		✓	✓		✓			✓	✓					✓		✓	✓	✓	✓	✓	✓		✓		✓	✓	✓	✓		
Problems w/ measurement	✓		✓	✓						✓			✓	✓	✓							✓	✓	✓	✓	✓		✓	✓	✓	✓	✓		✓		
Open-ended problems	✓				✓																✓						✓				✓	✓				✓
Reasonableness or accuracy of solutions		✓	✓		✓							✓			✓		✓					✓		✓			✓				✓	✓	✓		✓	✓

115

© Incentive Publications, Inc., Nashville, TN

INCENTIVE PUBLICATIONS DAILY PRACTICE SERIES
GRADE 5 MATH SKILLS

Geometry

Skill	1	2	3	4	5	6	7	8	9	10	11	12	13	14	15	16	17	18	19	20	21	22	23	24	25	26	27	28	29	30	31	32	33	34	35	36
Points, lines, line segments, rays, and planes		√	√	√		√								√			√	√						√				√						√		
Angles	√			√	√					√	√				√		√				√		√		√				√				√			
Identify plane figures				√					√	√									√		√	√		√	√			√					√	√		
Properties of plane figures	√		√				√			√										√	√	√	√	√	√			√	√				√	√		
Symmetry		√					√		√					√					√								√			√						√
Identify space figures		√			√						√					√	√						√		√	√			√				√			
Properties of space figures	√		√										√				√				√	√			√	√		√	√		√	√				
Similar figures			√								√		√			√						√					√			√					√	
Congruent figures			√	√				√										√						√												
Draw figures		√	√			√					√				√				√							√	√				√	√				
Coordinate graphs			√	√				√		√	√	√	√																			√				√

Measurement

Skill	1	2	3	4	5	6	7	8	9	10	11	12	13	14	15	16	17	18	19	20	21	22	23	24	25	26	27	28	29	30	31	32	33	34	35	36
Measurement units	√	√	√	√		√	√	√			√	√	√	√			√	√	√			√	√		√		√	√	√		√	√		√	√	√
Estimate measurements		√	√	√		√				√	√	√	√	√	√		√			√		√	√	√	√		√	√	√			√	√	√		√
Convert units	√	√	√	√	√		√	√	√		√	√	√		√		√		√		√	√	√	√	√		√	√	√		√	√	√	√	√	√
Angle measurements	√							√		√	√	√			√		√					√		√	√					√			√	√		√
Perimeter, circumference		√		√	√	√	√	√	√	√	√	√	√	√			√				√	√		√	√		√		√	√	√			√		√
Area of plane figures		√		√		√	√	√	√	√	√	√	√	√			√				√	√		√	√				√	√	√			√		√
Surface area (space figures)								√										√								√										
Volume of space figures															√						√		√				√		√	√			√			√
Temperature	√		√			√			√				√		√	√				√	√	√		√		√	√				√	√		√		√
Time	√	√				√	√	√	√		√	√	√	√	√	√	√	√	√	√	√		√		√		√	√	√		√	√	√	√		√
Weight			√		√		√	√			√	√								√		√		√		√	√		√	√	√			√	√	
Scale																						√				√							√		√	
Compare measurements	√		√	√	√		√		√	√	√	√	√	√	√		√		√	√	√	√		√	√		√	√	√				√			
Reasonableness/accuracy of a measurement								√		√				√			√	√		√	√	√		√	√		√		√			√		√		√

116

©Incentive Publications, Inc., Nashville, TN

INCENTIVE PUBLICATIONS DAILY PRACTICE SERIES
GRADE 5 MATH SKILLS

Statistics & Probability

Skill	1	2	3	4	5	6	7	8	9	10	11	12	13	14	15	16	17	18	19	20	21	22	23	24	25	26	27	28	29	30	31	32	33	34	35	36
Define statistical terms			√		√	√		√			√		√	√			√			√	√							√						√		
Interpret tables		√			√						√		√			√	√			√	√			√		√				√		√			√	
Find mean, range, median, mode in a set of data	√		√				√	√		√			√		√					√			√	√					√		√	√		√		
Select appropriate graph	√		√			√	√			√	√		√		√				√							√										
Interpret graphs	√		√		√	√		√			√			√	√	√		√			√	√		√					√				√	√		√
Solve problems from data	√		√		√	√							√	√		√	√			√	√	√		√	√	√			√	√	√	√				√
Translate data into a graph or table	√		√			√					√						√			√				√		√				√		√				√
Define probability terms			√		√												√																√			
Describe likelihood of an event	√								√				√	√	√	√				√			√													
Identify combinations									√					√					√							√										
Describe or count outcomes	√			√	√			√			√		√			√		√		√			√	√		√	√		√		√				√	
Find probability of one event		√		√	√		√		√		√		√		√	√							√	√	√				√		√				√	
Draw tree diagrams to show outcomes	√				√									√				√					√	√	√		√									
Find probability of two independent events								√			√					√				√		√		√						√					√	

INCENTIVE PUBLICATIONS DAILY PRACTICE SERIES
GRADE 5 MATH SKILLS

Pre-Algebra

Skill	1	2	3	4	5	6	7	8	9	10	11	12	13	14	15	16	17	18	19	20	21	22	23	24	25	26	27	28	29	30	31	32	33	34	35	36
Patterns and functions		✓	✓			✓		✓	✓		✓		✓	✓	✓			✓			✓		✓					✓	✓		✓					✓
Read and write expressions	✓				✓		✓			✓					✓							✓	✓					✓	✓		✓					✓
Simplify expressions			✓					✓			✓						✓			✓							✓			✓						
Match equations to problems		✓			✓	✓	✓				✓		✓					✓	✓						✓			✓								✓
Simplify equations				✓				✓			✓					✓								✓			✓									✓
Solve equations – one variable, one step	✓	✓	✓		✓					✓		✓														✓	✓			✓	✓					
Solve equations – one variable, multiple steps				✓					✓					✓		✓	✓			✓				✓					✓			✓			✓	
Given one variable, find a second one		✓				✓			✓							✓		✓			✓					✓						✓		✓		
Order of operations in equations			✓						✓		✓		✓				✓	✓				✓		✓				✓			✓			✓		
Verify accuracy of solutions		✓			✓		✓				✓								✓			✓			✓							✓				✓
Read and write inequalities					✓		✓		✓		✓				✓						✓				✓									✓		

118

© Incentive Publications, Inc., Nashville, TN

Week 1 (pages 5–7)

MONDAY
1. 741
2. 55
3. 11
4. Check to see that student drawings identify diameter properly.
5. $59.85

TUESDAY
1. b
2. 7
3. 94°F
4. 909
5. Answers will vary.

WEDNESDAY
1. a
2. 18
3. 908
4. 48 min
5. Draw FB, FC, FR, FM, BC, BR, BM, CR, CM, RM

THURSDAY
1. yes
2. a. 500; b. 200; c. 300
3. 444
4. a
5. number of members in the scout troop

FRIDAY
1. $150
2. 1751, 1715, 1175, 1157
3. 75
4. 480
5. a. 15%
   b. Check student graphs for accuracy.

Week 2 (pages 8–10)

MONDAY
1. 19 mph
2. 13.5
3. $\frac{3}{6}$ or $\frac{1}{2}$ OR 3:6 or 1:2
4. 11 p.m.
5. a. 5 (B, E, A, E, T)
   b. L, R
   c. no

TUESDAY
1. c
2. a number (y) times nine equals eighteen
3. 36 quarts
4. six hundred
5. 36 ft²

WEDNESDAY
1. a. 10; b. 20
2. 12.7
3. a
4. an octagon

5. a. 81 mph; b. 14 mph

THURSDAY
1. s = 25
2. 180 ft
3. 16
4. a. 0.25; b. 0.5; c. 0.75
5. a. Answers will vary.
   b. 5 hr, 10 min
   c. Answers will vary.

FRIDAY
1. $\frac{2}{3}$; $\frac{4}{6}$; lowest terms is $\frac{2}{3}$
2. 23
3. c
4. 90 cents
5. a. raisins: 3C   walnuts: 1C
      granola: 1C chocolate chips: 1C
      dates: 1$\frac{1}{2}$C sunflower seeds: 2C
      cashews: 1C cranberries: 1$\frac{1}{2}$C
   b. 3
   c. 24

Week 3 (pages 11–13)

MONDAY
1. a, b
2. a
3. three
4. 70 m
5. a. 2 cm; b. 6 cm; c. 4 cm

TUESDAY
1. $35
2. 28.56
3. Answers will vary: about 3 hours
4. 32
5. 36 in or 3 ft

WEDNESDAY
1. 300 lbs
2. a. 300 lb; b. 500 lb
3. a. 1,872
   b. Answers will vary depending on the current year; in 2011 = 139
4. 1530
5. c

THURSDAY
1. 7
2. 124
3. 2,200 yd
4. a
5. a. 900 ft; b. 585; c. $19

FRIDAY
1. no (Correct answer is $145.60.)
2. 6 p.m.
3. 78 mi
4. 18
5. a. Check student graphs for accuracy
   b. increasing by 7, 8, 9, 10, 11
   c. 233

Week 4 (pages 14–16)

MONDAY
1. b
2. 21
3. $\frac{5}{26}$. If y is counted as a vowel: $\frac{6}{26}$ or $\frac{3}{13}$
4. 1809
5. d

TUESDAY
1. 113
2. 18 ft²
3. 3
4. $32,499,720
5. a

WEDNESDAY
1. 108,324,972
2. 10:50 am
3. 123
4. $\frac{2}{7}$
5.

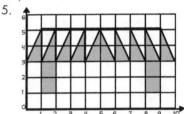

THURSDAY
1. 6.1 m
2. simplify to 6m; answer = 66
3. c
4. 9 m
5. 1 is Jiangyin; 2 is Humber; 3 is Great Belt; 4 is Izmet; 5 is Akashi–Kaikyo

FRIDAY
1. 8,000
2. d
3. nine
4. Check student drawings for accuracy.
5. Chelsea—6; Peter—18; Amber—25; Ben—40

Week 5 (pages 17–19)

MONDAY
1. They drank the same amount.
2. $\frac{8}{8}$ or 1
3. $\frac{4}{12}$ or $\frac{1}{3}$
4. Labels may vary. One possible answer: People who like apples and oranges.
5. a. can
   b. tomato
   c. half grapefruit
   d. cone
   e. box
   f. cheese

ANSWER KEY

TUESDAY
1. 32,104
2. d
3. >
4. 7¢
5. 2 lb, 8 oz

WEDNESDAY
1. d
2. $1\frac{1}{3}$ C
3. errors in tens column and ones column; correct answer is 444
4. 96 in^3
5. 110°

THURSDAY
1. $\frac{12}{6}$ or $\frac{2}{1}$ or 2
2. 5.7
3. 352
4. 34
5. yogurt – $1\frac{1}{2}$ C
   banana – 1 whole
   strawberries – $\frac{3}{4}$ C
   milk – $\frac{3}{4}$ C
   ice cubes – 12

FRIDAY
1. a. 50; b 335
2. 280
3. $\frac{90}{180}$; $\frac{1}{2}$; 50%
4. 5 gal
5. 8 different sandwiches possible: Combinations are: W, T, CC; W, T, SC; W, H, CC; W, H, SC; S, T, CC; S, T, SC; S, H, CC; S, H, SC

Week 6 (pages 20–22)

MONDAY
1. Answers will vary depending on the current year (199 in 2011)
2. 900 (approximately)
3. 68
4. 70°
5. Student problems will vary. Check for accuracy.

TUESDAY
1. 84
2. 2,190
3. identity property for multiplication
4. d
5. b

WEDNESDAY
1. 3^5
2. (3 + 2 + 4) is divisible by 3; answer = 108
3. −3°F
4. 39
5. Review student drawings for accuracy.

THURSDAY
1. 3,200,000 m
2. 36.2; 35.1; 34.06; 32.6; 30.48
3. 147
4. 100.48 in
5. M: 21; T: 25; W: 22; Th: 31; F: 33

FRIDAY
1. 16
2. a
3. 2 hr, 55 min
4. 3.17
5. Check student graphs to see that information has been entered correctly.

Week 7 (pages 23–25)

MONDAY
1. 4
2. <
3. Necessary information: Need to check in by 7:30 for flight; it takes 50 minutes to get to the airport.
4. 37.2 m
5. 126 in^2

TUESDAY
1. d
2. 9, 4, 15, 6
3. 2.35
4. 35, 29, 22
5. b, c

WEDNESDAY
1. 6
2. 2000
3. 39 (thirty-nine)
4. $\frac{1}{6}$
5. 44 cm

THURSDAY
1. 1,600
2. 300,000
3. a. 43; b. 58; c. 121
4. a
5. less than; more than

FRIDAY
1. about $12 or $13
2. $11.99
3. $3.01
4. 49¢
5. Chicago: arrive San Francisco 11:08 a.m.
   Portland: arrive New Orleans 6:17 p.m.
   Nashville: arrive Philadelphia 9:54 a.m.
   Charlotte: arrive Atlanta 2:56 p.m.
   Miami: arrive Los Angeles 5:23 p.m.
   Los Angeles: arrive Honolulu 12:05 p.m.

Week 8 (pages 26–28)

MONDAY
1. 2 hr, 45 min

2. 30
3. 96 in^2
4. congruent
5. a. Australia
   b. Germany and Hungary

TUESDAY
1. about 70
2. 6.4
3. Peter – 12; Pam – 6
4. A. 80°; B. 20°; C. 110°
5. Pairs from top to bottom: (5, 7); (3, 5); (6, 8); (9, 11); (10, 12)

WEDNESDAY
1. 5
2. a
3. x; ÷
4. 18
5. 18.84 m

THURSDAY
1. The boys' combined weights would probably exceed 75 pounds, so they should not use the raft together.
2. simplify to 5p; answer = 30
3. −3
4. $\frac{1}{3}$: H; $\frac{3}{5}$: H; $\frac{7}{8}$: W; $\frac{11}{12}$: W; $\frac{3}{8}$: H; $\frac{5}{6}$: W
5. a. Bubbles are at: (0, 3) ; (1, 2); (4, 1); (5, 2); (5, 6)
   b. Answers will vary

FRIDAY
1. 9 hrs
2. $6\frac{2}{5}$:
3. 2
4. 3 row across: 3, 6, 9, 12, 15, 18, 21, 24, 27, 30, 33
   4 row across: 4, 8, 12, 16, 20, 24, 28, 32, 36, 49, 44
   Multiples in common are 12, 24, 36
5. a. Check student drawings.
   b. There are a few ways to determine the deck area. For instance: Count the squares on the graph covered by the deck; find the area of the whole figure and subtract the area of the pool; divide the deck into sections and find the area of each, then add together. The area of the deck is: 512 ft^2
   c. 22
   d. $1098.90

Week 9 (pages 29–31)

MONDAY
1. 3
2. 18.929
3. a. l; b. ml; c. l; d ml; e. l
4. a. $\frac{3}{10}$; b. $\frac{10}{10}$

5. Check student drawings for accuracy.

TUESDAY
1. $156
2. 1 ft, 5 in
3. 24,697
4. 14
5. 1000; 10,000; 100,000
   The number of zeroes is equal to the exponent.

WEDNESDAY
1. 1,100
2. 12
3. 3 lb, 1 oz
4. *Thomas Edison Boy Inventor* and
      One Hundred Popular Inventions

   Thomas Edison Boy Inventor and
      Be An Inventor

   Thomas Edison Boy Inventor and
      The Age of Invention

   One Hundred Popular Inventions and
      Be An Inventor

   One Hundred Popular Inventions and
      The Age of Invention

   Be An Inventor and
      The Age of Invention
5. a. rhombus or parallelogram;
   b. parallelogram;
   c. square, rectangle, parallelogram or rhombus;
   d. rectangle or parallelogram

THURSDAY
1. $1,000,000
2. 26°
3. 47 hrs, 15 min
4. 18
5. c

FRIDAY
1. 120; 720
2. <
3. 9 cm
4. $\frac{6}{10}$; $\frac{9}{15}$; $\frac{15}{25}$
5. a. 8   e. 15.2 m   i. 13
   b. 12   f. 1,893   j. 21
   c. 204   g. 5,000,000   k. 84
   d. 172   h. 2,000
   Puzzle Answer: What a genius

Week 10 (pages 32–34)

MONDAY
1. b
2. 76.8
3. a. line; b. line segment; c. ray
4. c
5. 168 ft

TUESDAY
1. 45 − n = 18
2. 100,000 + 60,000 + 2,000 + 300 + 60 + 1
3. yes
4. 31
5. 27

WEDNESDAY
1. 347.1
2. a + 0 = a
3. 1,678
4. estimates may vary; actual = $3\frac{3}{8}$
5. a. 3; b. 4; c. 1; d. 2

THURSDAY
1. 576.3
2. no
3. 40
4. 1.32
5. b

FRIDAY
1. 194,940
2. −
3. a. $\frac{35}{100}$ or $\frac{7}{20}$; b. 0.35; c. 35%
4. 10
5. a. $159.50   c. Misty Falls Tours
   b. $ 172.80   d. $13.30

Week 11 (pages 35–37)

MONDAY
1. first and fourth figures
2. d
3. 6,282
4. 234 m^2
5. Possible combinations are:
   road bike (green) with light;
   road bike with mirror;
   road bike with both;
   mountain bike (black) with light;
   mountain bike with mirror;
   mountain bike with both

TUESDAY
1. Factors of 16 are 1, 2, 4, 8, 16;
   Factors of 20 are 1, 2, 4, 5, 10, 20;
   common factors are 1, 2, 4.
2. 10:13 a.m.
3. 1,270 estimate
4. 46
5. a. 59 − 56; 54 − 51; 49 − 46;
      44 − 41; 39 − 36; 34 − 31
   b. Each input number diminishes from the input number above it by 5.

WEDNESDAY
1. a. 37.68 in; 113.04 in; b. 75.36 in
2. Marna
3. a. 28; b. 34

4. Look at student figures to be sure each is a parallelogram.
5. a. (4, 2)
   b. (1, 5); (4, 6); (8, 2)

THURSDAY
1. =
2. 135,000
3. simplify to 4s; answer = 64
4. 3,000
5. a

FRIDAY
1. $1\frac{7}{8}$
2. b
3. a
4. 84 mi
5. There are many possible solutions; two examples: 36 bikes, 2 trikes, 5 unicycles OR 13 unicycles, 10 trikes, 20 bikes

Week 12 (pages 38–40)

MONDAY
1. 72°F
2. 7
3. 48.6 km
4. c
5. a. 2

TUESDAY
1. 35.06
2. a. 9°; b. 1.8°
3. b
4. approximately 70 T
5. 210 ft

WEDNESDAY
1. c
2. a
3. $\frac{7}{12}$
4. 16
5. a. 1958;
   b. Answers will vary depending on current year (53 years in 2011)

THURSDAY
1. 43
2. $\frac{5}{1}$ or 5
3. 63 × 1000 = 63,000
4. d
5. 40.575 kg

FRIDAY
1. 28.88
2. no; correct answer is 20.79
3. 10
4. $$22.75
5. Fiennes–1982; Steger–1986; Etienne–1986; Kazami–1987; Thayer–1988; Swan–1989

ANSWER KEY

Week 13 (pages 41–43)

MONDAY
1. 1,774
2. 30,000 lb
3. a. 33,333
   b. thirty-three thousand, three hundred, thirty-three
4. 6 faces, 8 vertices (points), 12 edges
5. Check student graphs for accuracy.

TUESDAY
1. b
2. 72 km
3. 20
4. $3.25
5. 648 in^2

WEDNESDAY
1. $\frac{2}{5}$ (Prime numbers — 2, 3, 5, 7)
2. incorrect; correct answer is $1\frac{3}{5}$
3. 74°
4. c
5. 7 in

THURSDAY
1. $1\frac{5}{12}$
2. a
3. 180
4. 66.64
5. c

FRIDAY
1. 15.5
2. $\frac{9}{18}$ or $\frac{1}{2}$
3. 15
4. 15.5
5. a. the number of shark attacks in 2002
   b. the number of bowls of soup sold on Saturday
   c. the shark population now
   d. the number of sharks in a school
   e. the length of the nurse shark now
   f. when the lemon shark lost its tooth

Week 14 (pages 44–46)

MONDAY
1. a. 20, 16
   b. 320 cm^2
2. 23 and 24
3. 84,524
4. Check student drawings for accuracy.
5. 184 km

TUESDAY
1. c
2. 80%
3. Simplify to 8r; answer is 88
4. a
5. a. 25, 25, 10
   b. $1.82

WEDNESDAY
1. d
2. b, c
3. 6
4. Check student drawings for accuracy.
5. d

THURSDAY
1. 38 ft
2. n = 28
3. 87.92
4. 352 mi
5. b

FRIDAY
1. 1900
2. 1941
3. 1994
4. 1996
5. Check student grids and coordinate lists to see that activity is done correctly.

Week 15 (pages 47–49)

MONDAY
1. b, c
2. rectangle
3. c
4. a
5. c

TUESDAY
1. $\frac{3}{5}$
2. <; >
3. a. 4,200 acres
   b. 100,800 acres
4. Missing output numbers: –2, 2, –3, –4
5. Range is 7 degrees (18–25)

WEDNESDAY
1. 2,800,000 m^2
2. 4.455
3. 77 yd
4. Check student drawings to see that trapezoid has been drawn.
5. $\frac{1}{4}$

THURSDAY
1. a. p – 16 = 6
   b. 21 + r = 25
2. 1 hr, 40 min
3. a
4. $3.50
5. Numbers for intersection of sets = 1, 2, 4

FRIDAY
1. 10^3
2. 19.5 ft
3. 23°F
4. 15.4 lb

5.

Week 16 (pages 50–52)

MONDAY
1. Check student drawings for congruency.
2. 1 min, 37 sec
3. a. 1,690; b. 16,900; c. 169,000
4. a. $\frac{1}{2}$; b. $\frac{1}{4}$
5. 258.85 k/hr

TUESDAY
1. a. $4\frac{1}{2}$;   b. $2\frac{2}{5}$
2. three
3. m = 7
4. approximate measurement: 41 mm
5. 8.84 million or 8,840,000

WEDNESDAY
1. 83.21
2. 1,700
3. Check student drawings for symmetry.
4. a. $\frac{6}{18}$ or $\frac{1}{3}$; b. $\frac{7}{18}$
5. Kyle: 7;   Quinn: 10;   Lane: 4

THURSDAY
1. 1,000 + 200 + 20 + 8
2. d
3. d
4. 240 km
5. b

FRIDAY
1. –4°F
2. 4 triangles, 4 parallelograms
3. $8550.00
4. nine thousand
5. a. 30 mi
   b. 1–2 hours
   c. about 200 mi
   d. no

Week 17 (pages 53–55)

MONDAY
1. a. 6   c. 4–9 (range of 5)
   b. 5.5   d. 4
2. 18.9224 (or 18.9)
3. 15; 45
4. a. rectangular prism   c. pyramid
   b. cube   d. cylinder
5. 252 in^2

TUESDAY
1. 53,116,043
2. $\frac{2}{5}$
3. correct
4. a. 63°;   b. 35°;   c. 12°
5. $3.83

WEDNESDAY
1. a
2. a. line;   b. ray;   c. line segment
3. pizza slice = $1.75; juice = $1.75
4. diameter = 11 in;
   circumference = 34.54 in
5. d

THURSDAY
1. a. $\frac{2}{3}$ b. $\frac{1}{2}$ c. $\frac{4}{5}$ d. $\frac{1}{3}$
2. 3.6
3. Simplify to 6m = 54; (m = 9)
4. 3 lb, 5 oz
5. a. approximately 30
   b. Check student graphs for accuracy.

FRIDAY
1.

2. 5:07 p.m.
3. 54.531
4. 13
5. a. flour = 294 C
      tomato sauce = 294 C or 18 gal,
      1 qt, 2 C
      mozzarella = 784 oz or 49 lb
      pepperoni = 392 oz or 24 lb, 8 oz
      Feeds approx. 390–400 people
   b. 15 in pizza: C = 47.1 in
      122 ft, 8-in pizza: C = 4622.08 in
   c. and d. Answers will vary.

Week 18 (pages 56–58)

MONDAY
1. c
2. 16,560 mi
3. 154, R 5
4. 13
5. a. parallel; b. perpendicular;
   c. intersecting

TUESDAY
1. a. Estimates will vary (about 110)
   b. 111.72
   c. answers will vary
2. $5\frac{5}{8}$
3. 64,997
4. Output column from top to bottom:
   9, 7, 6, 4
5. Check student work for accuracy.

WEDNESDAY
1. 8:16 a.m.

2. 5,100
3. 10^2
4. a
5. 6

THURSDAY
1. 51.85
2. 28°F
3. a. 63.1;   b. 0.1;   c. 12.5
4. 99 kg
5. B = (3, 2); A = (2, 4); L = (4, 5);
   L = (6, 5); O = (7, 2); O = (8, 4);
   N = (5, 1)

FRIDAY
1. 117 (S)
2. a. 312 (K);   b. 2.36 (Y)
3. a. 25 (H);   b. 15 (I)
4. a. 2.36 (G);   b. 0.54 (H)
5. a–c: Examine student products:
      pink = 7, blue = 2, yellow = 4,
      lavender = 2 , lime green = 6

Week 19 (pages 59–61)

MONDAY
1. 400,000
2. Check student
   labels for accuracy.
3. 19 R 6
4. 486 in²
5. 6 possibilities: WP, WC, WE, JP, JC, JE

TUESDAY
1. 7:47 a.m.
2. y = 45
3. b. subtraction
4. a. 190;   b. 1,900
5. a. 6: 12, 18, 24, 30, 36, 42, 48,
      54, 60, 66, 72;
      8: 16, 24, 32, 40, 48, 56, 64,
      72, 80, 88, 96
   b. 24, 48, 72
   c. 24

WEDNESDAY
1. Check student drawings for accuracy.
2. 9,678.33 or 9,678 yd and 1 ft
3. a
4. no; 2 yards for each square is far too
   large an amount
5. $12.50

THURSDAY
1. a and c (answer is 47°F)
2. a. 0.5;   b. 0.125;   c. 0.8;   d. 0.25
3. Check student drawings on number
   line. Answer is –6.
4. 17,320 ft
5. Answers will vary. One possibility:
   people who've climbed both
   Mt. Everest and Mt. McKinley

FRIDAY
1. 5548
2. c; Answer is 14
3. 9
4. 88.07% or 88%
5. a-d Answers will vary. Check student
   graphs and questions for accuracy.

Week 20 (pages 62–64)

MONDAY
1. c
2. 1
3. 55
4. Check student drawings (small hand
   should be about halfway between 3
   and 4; large hand on 9)
5. $\frac{2}{3}$

TUESDAY
1. $5\frac{11}{12}$
2. b
3. Answers will vary, depending on the
   current year (in 2011: 383)
4. 22
5. a. Dr. C = 26;
   b. Dr. R = 24;
   c. Dr. F = 8

WEDNESDAY
1. 4200; 100,800
2. 193.55
3. a
4. 3.8°F
5. a. 3 bpm (69 – 72); b. 71 bpm

THURSDAY
1. 574.52
2. 78,000
3. 503,300
4. 14
5. an hour: 180 qt (or 45 gal);
   a day: 4,320 qt (or 1,080 gal);
   a week: 30,240 qt (or 7,560 gal)

FRIDAY
1. 59
2. a. $\frac{3}{4}$;   b. $\frac{3}{10}$;   c. 6
3. a. 20: 1, 2, 4, 5, 10, 20;
      30: 1, 2, 3, 5, 6, 10, 15, 30
   b. 10
4. 5-inch height
5. Check student tables to see that
   students have organized the
   information. It might be organized
   by time or by heart rate.

Week 21 (pages 65–67)

MONDAY
1. $40.65
2. a. <; b. >; c. >; d. <

ANSWER KEY

3. 160,000 km^2
4. A = 160°; B = 85 °; C = 135 °
5. a. four degrees (−38° to −42°);
   b. 40°; c. 40°; d. 40°

TUESDAY
1. 12$\frac{3}{4}$
2. b
3. d
4. s = 3
5. Check student drawings. The dune should be 10 squares tall.

WEDNESDAY
1. a. kg; b. g; c. kg; d. mg
2. 50°
3. 197.12
4. 3 hrs, 11 min
5. a. 44 oz
   b. 11 a.m. and noon as between 9 and 10 a.m.

THURSDAY
1. −4
2. 9 in^2
3. 0.02; 0.022; 0.2; 2.2; 20.2; 22.2
4. fourth pattern should have four spines on the small part, and eight spines on the large part
5. c

FRIDAY
1. 300,000 mi^2
2. 17,612 mi^2
3. 9,100,000
4. total: $12.75; change: $37.25
5. Check student grids to see that path coordinates are correctly identified.

Week 22 (pages 68–70)

MONDAY
1. 6.2
2. A = 5; B = 6
3. 126.2 OR 126, R 7
4. 10 cm
5. a. 120; b. 120

TUESDAY
1. About 800
2. 4.25
3. 15.7 m
4. $\frac{3}{4}$; $\frac{7}{10}$; $\frac{1}{2}$; $\frac{2}{5}$
5. c

WEDNESDAY
1. b and d
2. correct
3. 2000 m
4. $\frac{12}{20}$ or $\frac{3}{5}$
5. a. W and N; b. I

THURSDAY
1. 36
2. (3 + 2) x 8 = 40
3. $\frac{1}{5}$ and $\frac{3}{15}$
4. −5 (Check student number line verifications.)
5. about 320 mi

FRIDAY
1. 15
2. addition
3. $\frac{1}{4}$
4. a. 0.25; b. 25%
5. #100: Smith, red house, boa;
   #102: Ruiz, white house, stop sign;
   #104: Bernstein, green house, cow;
   #106: McCall, brown house, bathtub

Week 23 (pages 71–73)

MONDAY
1. 75°
2. a
3. 42
4. 129
5. Two Branches (S and F); six branches (R, J, C and R, J, C); twelve branches (W, B on each pair); The number of possible combinations for her drawing is 12.

TUESDAY
1. 17,998.4 g
2. 8$\frac{3}{5}$
3. $\frac{12}{60}$ or $\frac{1}{5}$
4. Pattern is: times 3 plus 4; next two are 237, 241
5. d

WEDNESDAY
1. 7 hours
2. a. triangular prism;
   b. rectangular prism;
   c. pyramid with square base
3. 218,122
4. 3:10 p.m.
5. E and K, E and G, E and C, K and G, K and C, G and C

THURSDAY
1. 12, 15, 21, 6
2. 31 yd, 2 ft (or 32 yards)
3. $448
4. b = 7
5. $26.02

FRIDAY
1. n = 6
2. 112°F
3. seven thousand two hundred five
4. 92.5

5. a. Table completion:
   American Woodcock – 70 hrs – Friday 10:30 a.m.
   Crow – 14 hrs – Sunday 6:30 p.m.
   Eagle – 7 hrs – Monday 1:30 a.m.
   Falcon – 1 hr, 45 min – Monday 6:45 a.m.
   b. $\frac{200}{50}$ or 4; $\frac{5}{25}$ or $\frac{1}{5}$
   c. $234.00

Week 24 (pages 74–76)

MONDAY
1. c
2. 2$\frac{1}{12}$
3. a
4. a. $\frac{9}{15}$ or $\frac{3}{5}$; b. 60%
5. a. 1;   b. $\frac{2}{6}$ or $\frac{1}{3}$;   c. $\frac{1}{6}$

TUESDAY
1. fourteen thousand, seven hundred, fifty
2. 1$\frac{4}{5}$
3. a. 3;   b. 6;   c. 9
4. 3n = 15; n = 5
5. 960 in^3

WEDNESDAY
1. no
2. 7.85 in
3. 6900
4. Check student drawings for accuracy.
5. a. approximately 26 mph (15 to 41)
   b. June-July

THURSDAY
1. 45.68
2. a. 10,200 ft^2 b. 410 ft
3. b
4. 6 of 10; 60%
5. #2: 1000 mg;   #3: 2000 lb;
   #8: 2 U.S. tons;   #10: 336 oz

FRIDAY
1. Brazil: 17,200; U.S.: 12,650;
   Denmark: 4150; Australia: 2875;
   Germany: 2725
2. 4550
3. 10,000 + 7000 + 200
4. Check student graphs for accuracy.
5. Check student responses for accuracy.

Week 25 (pages 77–79)

MONDAY
1. a. 26 ft; b. 81.64 ft
2. <
3. 68.3
4. $\frac{2}{6}$ or $\frac{1}{3}$
5. frog (−2, 3); pine cone (3, 5);
   maple leaf (−6, 2); squirrel (5, 1)

124

TUESDAY
1. 1, 2, 4, 5, 8, 10, 20, 40
2. c
3. 9 cm
4. 200.96 in²
5. b, c, or d

WEDNESDAY
1. a & e
2. 163, R 20 OR 163.8
3. 287 ft, 6 in
4. 80°
5. $329.45

THURSDAY
1. c
2. 20
3. a. 59.6
   b. 24.9
   c. 40
4. Rule = Multiply input by a number that is one greater than used to multiply the previous input; 5 & 30; 6 & 42; 7 & 56
5. 7:36 a.m.

FRIDAY
1. a. On the second step, he forgot to move over one place to the left.
   b. 336
2. c
3. 5200
4. Examine student drawings to see that they are symmetrical and that a correct line of symmetry has been drawn.
5. a. Check student order blanks to be sure they have used $600 or less for their purchases.
   b. 66 days

Week 26 (pages 80–82)

MONDAY
1. a. 18; b. 9
2. $9\frac{5}{10}$ or $9\frac{1}{2}$
3. b
4. a
5. a. 18 cm
   b. approximately. 29 sq units (or 58 sq in)

TUESDAY
1. m = 7
2. 13° C
3. 44
4. 3,215,175
5. a. $0.84
   b. $7.60

WEDNESDAY
1. associative

---

2. 10 (MM, MB, MV, MS, BB, BV, BS, VV, VS, SS)
3. 112
4. 184 in²
5. a and g

THURSDAY
1. 3.25
2. p = 12
3. $8\frac{3}{6}$ or $8\frac{1}{2}$
4. 68
5. a. $\frac{2}{3}$
   b. $\frac{1}{2}$
   c. $\frac{1}{3}$

FRIDAY
1. Answers will vary.
2. 5.9 liters
3. Sweden, Finland, Australia, U.S., New Zealand
4. 3,740,000 liters
5. Answers may vary; one solution:
   Left row top to bottom: 5, 8, 3, 4;
   Right row top to bottom: 5, 7, 2, 6;
   Bottom row left to right: 4, 9, 1, 6

Week 27 (pages 83–85)

MONDAY
1. 92 years old
2. 33,820
3. c
4. Check student drawings for accuracy.
5. a. $\frac{1}{6}$
   b. $\frac{2}{6}$ or $\frac{1}{3}$
   c. $\frac{4}{6}$ or $\frac{2}{3}$

TUESDAY
1. $27.00
2. a
3. 1 ft, 3 in
4. 1,500,000
5. 5 hr, 50 min (not counting time between attractions)

WEDNESDAY
1. 144.44 in (or 12 ft, 0.44 in)
2. a
3. 1050
4. Tina
5. Check student drawings for accuracy.

THURSDAY
1. 8 x 10⁴
2. 13
3. thirty-three thousand, six hundred seventy-two
4. the price of the puzzle
5. 144

FRIDAY
1. 75%

---

2. $2\frac{5}{8}$
3. a. 3225
   b. The sum of the digits is divisible by 3.
4. c
5. Answers will vary. Two possibilities are: 1H, 10Q, 5D, 2N, 8P and 4H, 2Q, 10D, 2N, 8P

Week 28 (pages 86–88)

MONDAY
1. Clock b should read 5:50.
2. correct
3. Check student drawings for accuracy; equilateral triangle
4.
5. a: range; b: mean; c: median; d. mode

TUESDAY
1. 68%
2. –4
3. $\frac{3}{4}$
4. 60
5. b

WEDNESDAY
1. 8
2. c
3. 5
4. a
5. a. (–2, 6); b. (1, 9); c. (–4, 2)

THURSDAY
1. 400,000,000; 4 x 10⁸
2. incorrect; s = 126
3. 2502 ft
4. 12.86
5. a. 133 (counting the day of rescue)
   b. Answers will vary depending on current date.

FRIDAY
1. eighty or eight tens
2. 280,000
3. 9
4. $2.25 if there is a charge for the day the book is returned
5. Check to see that the following numbers are circled:
   a. 1,583   f. 1,391
   b. 484   g. 1,985
   c. 1,400   h. 1,616
   d. 400,000   i. 1,287
   e. 1,622   j. 1,510

Week 29 (pages 89–91)

MONDAY
1. 104

ANSWER KEY

2. 401,258
3. 89
4. a and d
5. 60 in or 5 ft

TUESDAY
1. 24
2. Estimates will vary; actual measurement: 5 cm
3. $\frac{6}{15}$ or $\frac{2}{5}$
4. 0.88
5. b; q = 8

WEDNESDAY
1. a
2. 214.19 or 214, R 7
3. 15
4. a. pyramid
   b. rectangular prism
   c. triangular prism
5. two

THURSDAY
1. c
2. a. 1800; b. 43,200
3. $\frac{2}{3}$; $\frac{3}{4}$; $\frac{7}{8}$
4. 152, 150, 600
5. 0 yds, 1 ft, 10 in

FRIDAY
1. 20,000
2. acute: b and d;
   obtuse: c;
   right: a
3. 2.6
4. $\frac{67}{73}$
5. Answers will vary. Check student tables for accuracy.

Week 30 (pages 92–94)

MONDAY
1. 1920 in^2
2. 2,700,000,000
3. $24.11
4. a. M, W, A, T; b. O
5. a. 133; b. No, because there were no world-wide radio broadcasts until many years after the first phone call.

TUESDAY
1. d
2. 80%
3. 9d = 54
4. 18
5. 432 in^2

WEDNESDAY
1. a and d
2. –3
3. 225 min or 3 hr, 45 min

---

4. 65°; 40°
5. a. 25°
   b. Answers may vary. Temperatures held fairly steady . . .

THURSDAY
1. d
2. 19.608
3. 36
4. 0
5. 14 cm

FRIDAY
1. 2,000,000
2. five hundred twenty million
3. $1\frac{1}{2}$
4. 225
5. a. Dwane: $115.75;
   Debbie: $208.35;
   Diane: $347.25;
   David: $191.50
   b. $862.85
   c. $37.10

Week 31 (pages 95–97)

MONDAY
1. 37.68 in
2. 6382
3. 11
4. b; It does not have two sets of parallel sides.
5. a. 9;   b. $\frac{1}{9}$

TUESDAY
1. d
2. 45 min
3. 0.014, 0.04, 0.14, 1.14, 1.4
4. 36°
5. 2200

WEDNESDAY
1. 501.6
2. incorrect
3. the amount the tourists spend; solution is 24.4 million 0r 24,400,000
4. a. 5;   b. 2;   c. 1
5. $\frac{2}{3}$

THURSDAY
1. 625
2. 48 oz
3. a. 4.01   b. 0.53   c. 0.01
4. a. Multiply 6 x 3 = 18;
   b. add 4 + 18 = 22;
   c. subtract 22 – 1 = 21
5. $32.80

FRIDAY
1. 8 hrs, 15 min
2. $6\frac{1}{15}$
3. 2 yd, 1 ft, 4 in

---

4. 24
5.

1	3	7	6	4	5	8	2	9
6	4	8	7	2	9	1	5	3
5	2	9	3	1	8	7	6	4
8	7	3	4	9	2	5	1	6
2	1	4	8	5	6	3	9	7
9	5	6	1	7	3	2	4	8
3	8	5	9	6	1	4	7	2
4	6	1	2	8	7	9	3	5
7	9	2	5	3	4	6	8	1

Week 32 (pages 98–100)

MONDAY
1. 1918
2. 227,264
3. 3419
4. a quadrilateral with two parallel sides and no right angles; Check student drawings for accuracy.
5. people who watched both the Lions game and the Lakers game

TUESDAY
1. 27
2. a. $\frac{1}{3}$;   b. $\frac{3}{4}$;   c. $\frac{1}{4}$
3. 23
4. d
5. a. 8100; b. 900

WEDNESDAY
1. 6
2. –8
3. 827
4. Estimates will vary; actual measurement: 3 cm
5. mitt (3, 5); bat (–3, 6); helmet (–2, –4); home plate (6, –2)

THURSDAY
1. 600 + 40 + 3
2. 5.6
3. 7
4. 42 in
5. Answers will vary.

FRIDAY
1. 67%
2. $5\frac{10}{21}$
3. 9
4. two thousand six hundred
5. Check student graphs for accuracy

Week 33 (pages 101–103)

MONDAY
1. a and d
2. 40,000,000
3. It is likely that it will rain twice during the week of June 3rd.
4. 6 possible combinations:
   Sears Tower–Hancock Observatory;
   Sears Tower–Field Museum;

Sears Tower–Aon Center;
Hancock Observatory–Field Museum;
Hancock Observatory–Aon Center;
Field Museum–Aon Center

5. 120°

TUESDAY

1. Answers will vary depending on the year (in 2011: 12 decades)
2. a. 3
   b. 5
   c. 7
3. d
4. d
5. c

WEDNESDAY

1. Answers will vary according to current date; in 2011: 8,000 times
2. $3\frac{1}{6}$
3. 11:35 a.m.
4. a. Check student drawings for an accurate acute angle.
   b. Check student drawings for an accurate obtuse angle.
5. a. 105; b. 15

THURSDAY

1. 20
2. correct
3. 16.5
4. 4.608 (or 4.6)
5. 48

FRIDAY

1. 5,025 and 1,680; These numbers each end in zero or five.
2. 800
3. a. T; b. F
4. $4.15
5. Students' skyscrapers will vary. Check to see that directions were followed, and that students have created a reasonable scale, using it to accurately calculate the height of the skyscraper.

Week 34 (pages 104–106)

MONDAY

1. 7,200,000 or 7.2 million
2. $7\frac{1}{2}$
3. 49 min
4. 65.94 ft
5. Check student drawings for accuracy.

TUESDAY

1. 4
2. a

---

3. 53 kg
4. $\frac{1}{5}$;

5. e

WEDNESDAY

1. b
2. 28°
3. The pattern is: The first number is multiplied by 1 to get the second number. The second number is multiplied by 2 to get the third number. The third number is multiplied by 3 . . . and so on. Missing numbers are 120, 720, 5040.
4. a. sphere   b. cone   c. cylinder
5. a. 5
   b. no; Some students may have checked out more than one book.

THURSDAY

1. 5
2. $\frac{1}{20}$
3. $3\frac{9}{20}$
4. 34.98
5. $637.50

FRIDAY

1. $10,000,000
2. 46
3. 1 min, 59 sec
4. 1875
5. a. 557 m^2
   b. two
   c. $75.90

Week 35 (pages 107–109)

MONDAY

1. b
2. 150,000
3. 9.6 mi
4. a and d
5. There are 8 possible combinations: SGO; SGW; SFO; SFW; JGO; JGW; JFO; JFW

TUESDAY

1. 16 yrs
2. 30
3. 644 yd
4. $\frac{1}{3} + \frac{2}{4}$ or $\frac{2}{4} + \frac{1}{3}$
5. a $(n + 7) \times 4 = 40$
   b. $n = 3$

WEDNESDAY

1. 60
2. –9
3. 54,864

---

4. $\frac{1}{9}$
5. 280 m

THURSDAY

1. <
2. 37 min
3. no; answer is 3
4. c
5. no

FRIDAY

1. 0.012; 0.112; 0.12; 1.2; 10.02
2. $23\frac{1}{10}$
3. Circle around 24, 14, and 21; box around 17, 2, 3, 11
4. 320
5. a. Seniors: 25; Adults: 30; Kids: 15; under 5: 5
   b. $1210.00

Week 36 (pages 110–112)

MONDAY

1. In 2011: estimate—about 1209
2. 6
3. 34.2
4. Check student drawings for accuracy.
5. Check student tables for accuracy.

TUESDAY

1. 600,073,693
2. Simplification: 5v = 50; v = 10
3. 4.2
4. a. 12
   b. 288
5. 792 in^2

WEDNESDAY

1. 1,500,000
2. distributive
3. Answers may vary; a bar graph
4. Estimates will vary; actual length: 6.8 cm
5. Check student grids for accuracy.

THURSDAY

1. yes
2. $\frac{3}{4}$
3. 24
4. (4, 2); (2, 0); (1, –1); (0, –2)
5. 116 (Note that the corner roses should not be counted twice.)

FRIDAY

1. 27.75
2. 6
3. 140
4. 16
5. Solutions will vary. One possible solution: single—25; double—34; triple—15